Mirror of Refining Insight

Mirror of Refining Insight

An Introspective Look At Pursuing Your Purpose

M. A. Grayson

JM Merrill
PUBLISHING

Contents

J Merrill Publishing, Inc.
434 Hillpine Drive
Columbus, OH 43207
www.JMerrill.pub

Library of Congress Control Number: 2021924436
ISBN-13: 978-1-954414-37-2 (Paperback)
ISBN-13: 978-1-954414-36-5 (eBook)

Book Title: Mirror of Refining Insight
Author: M. A. Grayson

PREFACE

Attentive Ears brings clarity into your unfulfilled Soul

Pain, rejection and disappointments - always untimely and you probably think too often.

Your Place in life, a mystery lost in clusters of ups and downs, not just in children.

True love, to most an elusive desire, seldom experienced, and if found, it's temporal?

Peace, sought by many, especially in times of restlessness, is seldom located.

Fairness, what all want to receive consistently, but seldom deliver, reasons for that too.

Don't Let Life Pass You by and You haven't found or fulfilled your Purpose

In all you accomplish, be an Inspiration. Strive to be the best you can be and that may take motivating yourself when others don't have anything positive to say about you?

As leaders – have you been motivated, or should your focus be motivating, and how so?

Maybe your life has been like the dog that chases his tail; when you get your goal completed, the void and restlessness remains?

When many are depressed, having pity parties, worrying about things they have little or no control over, instead of staying focused on the goal to be accomplished and what it takes to get there t's essential to appreciate your blessings, including achieved goals and also a great time to reach out and help or encourage others.

So, with that in mind, you have to keep it fresh on your mind, staying focused on the good that you've experienced and your goals, at times it is a daily pick me up.

Slow down. Time to get your Focus in alignment with some of these changes!

In agreement with my purpose, I submit emotionally motivating poems to remind you, refresh and enlighten you that life is about more than what you accomplish, even though accomplishments are necessary. All of you have goals you desire to meet in life and standards you must recognize and maintain. Hard to accomplish much without directions or aspirations! Your life needs structure and organization! We see children without self-awareness raised by parents with no integrity. No future, little hope, no goals and no idea that the lights are on. Just surviving the jungle of life, they hope? Lost in existing?

These are just a few of the topics with suggestive remedies that'll generate a smile or tear, which you'll find in this book. Amazing the magnitude of a timely, kind word.

Without standards, you have no integrity and an example might be the habit of persistence to give your best effort in all you do. The question is, do you finish? That's a reflection on who you've become and those who you associate with. Fairness is another good habit to develop because it's a component in developing prudence and loyalty. Another good trait is being proactive and responsible for what you say and do. Some call it being accountable.

Put first things first, utilizing discipline to prioritize today's work for pleasure later.

There is great satisfaction in completing and accomplishing goals that motivate you to pursue higher goals and it encourages others as they see your success. The more you accomplish, the better position you put yourself in to be a bigger inspiration.

These are just a few concepts and concerns that will be addressed with examples in the upcoming pages and may the depths of them help you find yourself, freedom and peace.

May the proactive voice enter the doorway to your open-minded soul to illuminate the dark places, providing clarity to escape and develop a more refined you.

CHAPTER 1

FEELINGS, NOT HAPPENINGS

Sitting on top of the world with disregard for those people.
Back to back, plus more questions in searching
Personal questions for personal edification
Always for your, excuse me, enjoyment and comfort.

Coming down to earth
And still, the inquisitive minds are out of sorts.
Folks trying to satisfy themselves, progressively wanting more.
Even if it ruins your world and opportunities.

Yeah, sitting on top of the world
Avariciousness has robbed and decimated so many.
And the right is deprived of Equality, not a concern even if you pay.
But that won't stop the sun from shining, but they're working on it.

As I sit on top of the world
And you bask in your enjoyment
May you enjoy eternally, at others' expense?
For now, their world may seem dim, but in time their lights will come on.

Chapter 2

Drive

As they presented verbal accolades of Thanks,
For my satisfaction's common denominator
Is the impartial universal opportunity, so my response was, No thanks.
And that's when they all laughed, which required an ear.

Achievements, despite how Great
Are only as good as the number of eyes that are thereby opened to see
The number of hearts that are encouraged and motivated to spin Right
The number of those that escape the vacuum
Through a relentless pursuit of the so-called "American Dream".

Shredded the opportunities to master many projected professions,
To be an unintentional, but chosen trailblazer.
Which would have gone unnoticed
Had they not removed the torch from my grasp?

Despite my successful completion of the early bitter tasks,
As I was willing to perform all the unwanted assignments,
While eating the crumbs off the floor,
But I appreciate, I was able to dine.

Look inside, Look inside yourself, dearest,
Dig deep and look inside with impartial undivided perception,
Because the amount of your growth is partially dependent on
How deep you dig to expel the odious in exchange for becoming virtuous.

Being dedicated to being the best you can be will present obstacles to hurdle.
An example in negating stereotypical barriers assigned,
The mental means of limiting success by binding others:
Personally, not succumbing, knowing the sky doesn't stunt your growth?

Didn't anyone ever educate you about assigned understood restrictions?
That used to be you can't do that and you don't have the ability to do this,
Then would follow up with what you could become by their dearth of choices?
You're not qualified or educated enough.
Lift up your head in spite of the disapprovals of rejection.

So, are you a man or a mouse? For no man wants to be a mouse.
But your level of humility forces you to vote
To be seen as a mouse is to accept others' limitations!
Being proactively constructive is to defy the odds, Drive.

CHAPTER 3

FAKE MYSELF OUT

Looking at life's past activities.
Feeling and participating in today's struggles.
Sightseeing on the future's fantasies,
I get the boogie fever.

Not knowing of myself tomorrow.
Not knowing if there will be a tomorrow.
I find myself wandering away.
As I fake myself out.

In a world unknown,
I see a determined people.
Determined to work to make life comfortable,
For a God-blessed future.

For if God doesn't bless it
And if we are not determined
And if we are not we-united,
Then there won't be much of a future.

M. A. GRAYSON

If you're not going to do it Right for yourself,
Yours, those that you care for and their neighbor.
Then the walls are about to fall on your house
I'd like to fake myself out, indefinitely.

CHAPTER 4

BROKE, BROKEN, YET CONTENT

Experiences, events, expressions and the lack of with attitudes do at times convey,
Busted or trusted, a way of shaping our lives and outlook on tomorrow.
The building fabric of who we allow to be a part of our lives and who we send up
the road.
The dialogues that create expectations on various levels and, in many, only the
peripheral.
Expectations that we feel confident in pursuing or laughing at as a forest for the
other guy.

I grew up in the Black and White two-channel TV days, when there weren't
remotes.
No cell phones, video games which left the only option as they suggested, go
outside and play.
Regardless of the weather, when children gathered, it was either fun, win or lose or
run from trouble,
That running helped us learn where bad decisions would take you in conjunction
with home lessons.
Daily chores encouraged responsibilities and disciplines that we didn't realize were
contagious.

Building personal foundations that develop into habits, good or bad, hopefully
with some accountability
As it helped us mature to make wise quality decisions, career-wise or personal,
broke or broken
That one day, we can gravitate to accept ourselves, regardless of how we dealt with
the storms.
To be at peace in having little or much and how to sort between the various outside
influences
To be comfortable with ourselves, without the need to justify our convictions or
way of living.

Having no room for trying to impress or live to any other standards than what's set
for me
Comfortable in my skin, my truth and history, appreciating the seeds of genuine
concern planted
Reaching out only to those in need that crave balance, clarity and inner peace, what
was sown in me
Because I know the ramifications of being judged incorrectly, but I'm at peace with
me, even content.

CHAPTER 5

EXPLOITING THE BABY

Valuable experiences teach us that we learn more from our misfortunes,
Being at a loss, then from a penthouse stay, testing our limits and patience.
Advice that negates the paranoid night sweating from electing substance over
nobility.
Not to justify, but under duress, desperate times may require desperate measures.
But to many, duress is a distorted frame of mind to justify thievery, but not you.

The subtle ways of taking advantage of people, institutions and the government,
Cheating them out of what was set up for the underprivileged, justifying our
motives in, they owe me.
It's really mine that has become the slogan of conniving for thriving exploitation
groups.
The affluent and underachievers fighting their way up the ladder of deceit,
Where inconsideration and inconvenience overwhelms the thoughtful and stoic.

Far too often overlooked is the fact that a rapacious person overindulges in more than food.
Occasionally offering a trinket from the indurated in exchange for a generous return.
Every day simple decency and courtesy is usually foreign to their priorities,
As they make uncouth demands of others that they can't perform, nor would consider.
As I witness many that contend with disasters, humbling events and losses,
Making for tough lessons learned in adjusting their priorities from hoarding to surviving.

CHAPTER 6

THAT'S NOT ME

That dead silent moment where you're described differently than what you thought.
Trying to figure out why you never saw yourself that way, or are you misunderstood again?
Denying the realities of honest visual truths that send you home questioning your motives.
Your value system is magnified under the bright night lights that shake your emotional world.
Is that really me, or can I proceed to start frying bigger fish?

Who doesn't this describe, like a house without closets, yet claim transparency?
Words and actions you can't walk back and reasons only validated with shallow realities.
From all they claim familiarity in knowing that type of person, only to unplug from,
Especially when they're part of the same group, in admiration of their positions.
Life's friendly persuasions to follow wrong convictions to get to an appealing destination.

Claiming that's not what they said, knowing that's what they meant.

Claiming that's what they said, when that's not what they meant, truth be known?

Clarifying with cloudy sentiments and expressions to dispel the slightly distorted truth

Targeting the vulnerable, those who witnessed the harvest of bad seeds planted

Exercising restraint from their dubious habits, defining their refining, now that's not me, moment.

Those expressions you don't see in the mirror can trouble more than what you only see!

CHAPTER 7

THE TRANSPARENT MOVING TOUCH

Position yourself and prepare for this stunning announcement
Then again, getting the message when prepared isn't always?
Things we want to hear – matters we'd love to experience
Tasting the unexpected often brings bitterness to the sweets.

Who have I touched, or is it how have I touched?
I have felt their pains and witnessed their dismay
I have been skilled to see beyond their attire and expressions.
No need to dig and I have no inquiries to request.

No, I'm not going into the insignificant, but I will assure you
You haven't arrived and your efforts have been so self-serving
But as we regroup to regain our true focus, notice I did say True
I can't help but notice and prescribe; reciprocation isn't required.

Ok, maybe that's a bit strong and we have been appreciative
But as denial has driven society to succumb to excessiveness
And as Generation Dust reaches blindly for the graveyards,
We experience things we don't want to hear and matters we wish not to see.

An empty promise and another call never returned
But you are never alone and your heart has been read, even the gray matter.
Yet, a great development comes in following your heart.
As you watch the nothingness of every day, all a part of a vicious cycle.

The unexpected timely reception, elusive expression says so much more
Like a fresh inhalation of one that's had the breath knocked out.
And they say no one likes to do windows,
Now we see how we've missed the boat, the plane and the point.
So, I smirk, but now in amazement of stumbling over a simple truth.

Chapter 8

Reach Out

From the eyes of an infant,
Comes the cries, the needs, just daily necessities
Wanting and calling you to fulfill.
But you respond with a shrug and I'll get to it.

From the eyes of the innocent,
Comes the cries, the desire yearning
Asking for your love and protection.
But I know, you just don't have the time right now.

From the eyes of a child
Comes the cries, a hunger, a craving
For your undivided attention, directions and some understanding
I have it to give but at my convenience.

From the eyes of a juvenile
Comes the cries, attempting to mature in looking for guidance
Getting rejection from the resourceful, acceptance from the depraved.
As we watch them drown in society's lost sinkholes.

Unfortunately, prejudgment causes us to call them hopeless,
Or is it just a label for nobody really cared enough or showed interest?
From their eyes, read them, if you're not too preoccupied to look up
Their undeveloped latent is enveloped, never nourished for lack of reach.

Chapter 9

The Crowd behind Me

It's getting late and chilly
And I'm starving, in case you didn't know.
So, as I boarded the bus for home
I sat down in the front row.

Just two blocks into the journey
I started to fall asleep
Then noticed voices conversing behind me
As I felt someone pushing me.

So, I looked back into the crowd
At the one directly behind me
Inquiring, had he just pushed me?
When he responded with a, No!

That's when I realized, at some point in time,
Including yesterday,
Whether abrasive or subtle and often more than once:
We all get pushed and pulled in some insightful way.

By a word said, direct or indirect.
A gesture made, distant or personal.
An expression, an event, a melody, a confrontation,
A relationship, an escapade, or through networking.

All do motivate in some way or fashion
Knowing the tougher the job, the greater the reward.
For there's development and growth in overcoming obstacles.
And the final product is reflective of the attitude it's assembled in.

Feels like someone's pushing me again as I follow the lead.
Oh, my stop! Time to wake up, get up and dismount.
The crowd behind me was initiating a progressive pursuit
Being prepared for what's coming from the front seat perception.

CHAPTER 10

A NOOSE IN OUR HISTORY

Regardless of their Win – Loss record
Every Team doesn't want a ringer.
Yes, they want to win.
But only under their conditions
Whether legal, ethical, or not?

Make a stand and walk the talk
Take advantage of the opportunities afforded you
But even in your defense,
The noose is in your history.

Educational challenges, Overcome.
Occupational opportunities, Devour.
Social issues, Silent them.
Doing it all for the team.
But are you doing it for, don't you look good?

Some see you as a misfit but wouldn't tell you
Many treat you as an outcast, unbeknown to you
Never contemplating the strength it takes
In swimming upstream under such frigid conditions.

M. A. Grayson

Not just for one day, but a lifetime.
A lifetime of minimal, if any, support.
A lifetime of minimal, if any, genuine encouragement.
A lifetime of minimal, if any, appreciation.
A lifetime, was it, has it been that long?

But my eyes and ears stay on alert
Just waiting for the seldom, Welcome being ingenuous
A welcome that comes with a price
Swimming upstream under frigid conditions.

That noose has no influence to many, oh so forgotten
Whether it should or not, maybe motivate?
To both the recipients and the inflictors
We're sure we've all been influenced by
The noose in whose history?

CHAPTER 11

THE POWER OF THE LIGHT SWITCH

You really don't recognize your power to influence others?
No, you really don't know!
No, you really don't appreciate all its value if you'd give it a voice?
Yes, you take it for granted, don't you?

You really don't utilize your power to influence positively enough?
No, you really don't
No, you don't appreciate all the love it channels, not just for your kids
But you expect your words of discouragement and correction to take full effect.

You really haven't been exercising discipline in influencing for good?
No, you really haven't! Not as much as you can.
No, you don't appreciate all the life it can give?
A slight oversight, or more like a casual dispersant.

You really don't allow your influences to flow, except on sunny days?
No, you really haven't without preference?
No, but you have the power to reverse and change all that now!
Forget yesterday, for today offers many new opportunities.

You really haven't allowed your influence to maximize.

No, you haven't; not realizing apprehension delays your approach and quiets their worry.

No, you didn't see this coming and definitely didn't expect it, hoping for a second chance?

But the same influence that has set you free is in you, to set others free.

The power of the light switch is your wake-up call.

Time to turn it on and just leave it on.

CHAPTER 12

AMAZES ME

Year In and year out, even though the clock I never give much attention
Time passes me by like I'm stuck in time
But one thing seems ever so apparent
I'm bombarded more by questions than I can answer
Just Amazes Me.

Tick, tock, tick, tock and day by day
The contributions to life, to others and to the unknown, for Pete sake
Seldom result in flowers and that's the sweetness of it all
Yet the mouth of the baby birds continue to crave for more
Just Amazes Me.

Over and over and again and again – denying foresight
Like the carrousel of life and the merry go round
Ignoring the call, or are you really just in denial
Hate the purpose if you want, you're still aware of the draw
Just Amazes Me

Your cycles in full operation, including your place of peace
Brings solutions and resolutions evolved out of revelations
But often provides more answers yet generates more inquiries
Yet for the I in pride and a blindfold
Many rather stumble in the darkness and be led to the slaughter
Just amazes me.

Chapter 13

Existing to Persist

Raised in the dirt, an old but real definition of humility.
But raised to be clean.
Love influences from one side
And dogs eat from the other.
It's the Rough life.

Seen death in so many ways, all not physical,
An early occasional gift of encouragement,
But far more impressions of suppression.
Just the typical day in the life of
The Minority life.

Those that would help me are down to Zero.
Those that would motivate me are gone.
Those that would pick me up are lost in their own struggles.
Those that would raise me are seeking their own refuge in
The Deprived life.

Finally, I found some support that life eradicated
And when I would get overdue supplements, love took that away.
Saw encouragement coming, but the streets snuffed them out.
Love reached out to rescue me and then insecurities made it withdraw in
The Reformed life.

M. A. GRAYSON

Now with few avenues of fruition opening-up
And the rivers of love flowing a little more reliably,
Surprisingly the support of many still is at a few
Brings tears to my eyes, seeing the fullness of evolution arise.
Just being able to see the sun set another day in
The Good Life.

CHAPTER 14

PRIORITIZED YOU

Stretching out in persistence to find what's appropriate
Finding the perfect fit, the ideal match
The elusive catch that defines my truth
How could I miss that recognizable face in the mirror?
That was supposed to be me.

Reaching for the one thing
And only coming up with one thing
But that one thing was more of what I needed
Than the one thing that I thought I needed
That was supposed to be, other than me.

As I awaken and without a search, I find
What was for me was more of an enlightenment of me
And the enlightening came when I knew
I was sure of it all with confidence
That there was a lot more to me than just me.

Glazed over eyes and with scattered thoughts
Confusion has attempted to make a temporal home
And my agenda no longer is as clear
Yet I remain sure as I walk
Knowing what I was, is no longer me.

M. A. GRAYSON

Taking a deep breath and taking a sip
Doing what comes naturally to regain clarity
The redefining of a new or is it just refined
Much appreciation to the realism of the truly dedicated
As I come to grips, in all its painfulness, that was supposed to be me.

CHAPTER 15

JUST NOT EASY, BEING ME

Things seem to flow ever so smooth
Good times put a smile on their faces
Success puts an extra pep in their step
A fresh new relationship revives a down heart.

Folks betting their lunch money on a chance at the lotto
But we all know life's a gamble
me take the risk to excel or die
The rest just watch in complacency, criticize and die.

Survivors see the risk as an opportunity, maybe even a challenge
A half-full glass to them is a Full glass when put in a cup
So, they high step and walk fast
Because they're excited about the optimistic outcome.

Put in a hard day's work and a full night of brainstorming
Even when many start so far in advance, yet have little opportunity
Recognizing the value of persistence and excellence
All for the pie a la mode in the sky.

M. A. Grayson

Some call it a competitive spirit
Some call it being stubborn or bullheaded
But I can appreciate your determination
Because it's just not easy being me or keeping up this pace.

CHAPTER 16

THAT'S THE NAME THEY CALL YOU

I'd rather walk in pain and excel beyond your limits
Then be allowed to spread my wings in a box
Or sell them for a quarter and for what?
To walk alone or at least without much support.

But then again, support comes when you have achieved
Support comes along with admiration after you've excelled.
But some stands you will have to make alone!
Some you will make when no one understands, nor concurs.

Many make choices for their best interest
Many make choices led by their fears and doubts
Many make the safe call and the favorite picks for personal gains
But I'd rather walk in pain and excel beyond your limits.

It's sad to see the discouraged hearts that was aflame to make this walk
That desire to walk in the knowledge beyond your finite learning
That knowledge that your parents tried to teach you with foresight
That knowledge that exceeds common, yet gets thwarted.

Many walk in fear,
But the fear of accepting your place and making priceless calls
Is the big hurdle that most never arrive
Because they get tripped up on the small nuisances, the trivial.

So even if I have to walk alone, often without support.
I will walk, even in pain, often deaf to exceed your limits.
Because I have to do this and will, even if you see me as difficult or aloof.
Knowing your support is based on an agreement and experience.

But it's hard enough for you to accept your place and purpose
I have no issues accepting mine, whether you comprehend it or not.
But one thing we both know is when you make a stand and walk
Many will never call you one of them because That's the name they call you.

CHAPTER 17

PANCAKES OR PANACEA

The benefits of being bland
Some prefer the spices of life to enhance.
A touch of this and a dab of that
Just to make life a little more exciting.
But the reserves would be content with just peace and tranquility.

Goals of this exploration tend to remain in flex
Others stay the same, but it's the players that are perplexed.
The tooth and nail fight to excel and accomplish
As the closet dwellers' desire is to effortlessly attain.
So, they can reside in a false shelter free of inconveniences and no blame.

Aspirations for all will continue to vary
A lot will remain lukewarm and settle for seventh place
Then you have the movers and the risk-takers
And just to think, it's often about a lifestyle, career, or relationship
Just to name the evasive few.

Driven by the mind over matter, if your mind matters
Then the emotional concerns get a vote too
Strategies influenced by the ultimate plan
Which is perfect, or is it perfect only for you?
Going through the motions and disciplined challenged.

M. A. GRAYSON

Plans with your best health issues in mind.
In mind of your heart, soul, body, and pursuits
The natural will need to take a seat for now.
whether you're riding or driving,
Just get in line for Pancakes or Panacea.

CHAPTER 18

YOUR TURN TO BE HEARD

They just don't understand you?
For some evasive reason, they can't comprehend your depths.
How many times do you have to say it?
And you've explained it over and over again.

Now that I have your attention
And I realize you attest to the former and you've been there?
I concur; understanding not only requires an attentive ear
But also a patient, objective mind.
A person that's been seasoned by the fires of pain and abuse.

See, I feel your pain through an osmotic sensitivity
But much of that is precipitated via your release to be set free.
How often have we tried to walk in others' shoes because they look nice?
Yet we judge blindly and counsel insensitively.
The power of the audio is greater than the volume of the vocal.

What will you sacrifice for your progressive emotional development?
Is there a worthy replacement for the maturation of your heart?
Then there are the remnants of us that seemed to have been lost in sensitivity
Acting like we've been raised by a pack of wolves
Or maybe we rather stay lost on lockdown in our own self-centered box?

Teachings and disciplines learned in discouraging manners and through painful experiences.
Disciplines and teachings taught in encouraging ways.
Will the cream come to the top in deliverance?
Or will fortitude without direction swallow up another?
Just shut up and listen for a moment.
You may need the same next?

CHAPTER 19

MY PERFECT WORLD IS REALLY IDEAL

Doesn't it amaze you how most desire to live in a perfect world
Often not thinking through, what's perfect for me
Doesn't equate into what's perfect for others; then again, guess that's your problem?
But that's the world we live in and how voting is applied indifferently.
But they try to give you what's their best and in ten will complain about it.

I repeat, what's most suitable for you
In all probability it isn't most suitable for your neighbor.
How you react in a given circumstance
Maybe be the complete opposite of what the next lady does.
You do know the different strokes policy of 1972?

The perfect world is a great aspiration and goal
But seeing how it incorporates others outside my island
Some tweaking and improvising becomes imperative
Especially when you intend to see this through fruition
Or be like the excuse-laden majority on the whiners' bench.

Your expression of beauty is viewed differently by your listeners than you intended
Your expression of love is interpreted differently by your family.
Your expression of discomfort is not understood in the same light it's given in.
Your passions and priorities are in disarray to me,
But I realize that's what works for you and doesn't make you wrong.

I also noticed, ouch can reflect the pain one gets in tolerating
When they can no longer justify their failures, or is that accountability?
Some will conveniently bend the rules and focus on pointing out others' miscues.
Turn a deaf ear and live in denial over the same guilty verdict they appoint.

Learning to accept and appreciate differences in the real world without criticizing
Is a big, refined step in living peaceably, if you really care?
Truth be known, living in a perfect world is more appropriately stated as
Living in my perfect world, or should I write, living in my ideal world.
There is a perfect world for you, but it may require some personal reconstruction.

CHAPTER 20

THE LIMB OF PERSUASION

I had worked far more than my shift and was exhausted
As I dismounted my piece of heavy equipment
I noticed out of the corner of my eye, a co-worker started back peddling.
I thought he may not realize he's about to back into trouble if he doesn't stop.

I hollered to get his attention or anyone near him, to no avail.
There were a few laborers near him, but they were caught up in their own world
Despite my continued efforts to get their attention, as I ran towards him in hast
He stepped backward and fell off a steep bank into a big lake, "splash".

As I continued to run to the lake, I realized those guys saw him the whole time
I dropped the belongings I had in hand alongside the bank
This worker sunk like a big rock as I looked for something to reach him
The laborers continued to laugh in hysterics.

I walked down to where he submerged with a tree branch in hand
None of the others ever got out of their seats
That's when the guy finally resurfaced, drowning and gasping for air
I jumped in with a stick in my hand and reached towards him.

His hands immediately grabbed the limb for dear life
I pulled the limb and him up onto the bank, where he arose safely, coughing
As I climbed up the bank, I saw the others had never moved
That's when it all hit me as clear as yesterday.

Everyone doesn't have that blend of active concern, persuasion and charity
On a day when most get lost in their own precedence
And the remnant just get caught up or lost in their own race
Just to contemplate how those two go hand in hand, another casualty has
occurred.
That's when I woke up and ascertained that resolving contributions requires
making an effort.
Just sad to think, there are way too many activities; more important is how they
roll?
Wake up!

CHAPTER 21

PAINFUL TRUTHS

You really need to get a hold of yourself!
Maybe step back and evaluate your thought process?
Maybe step back and critique your priorities?
Blame others if you want, but you have to be accountable; at some time?
Of course, if denial is where you rather reside, that's not you; read on.

Hearts want to experience the lavish life and prefer to negate the nadir.
Pockets want to enjoy the prosperous season and avoid the lean.
Egos want to hear the paeans and read accolades but be gone before the tide turns.
Such is life or life and death, and they go hand in hand, except during fair weather.
Now we're about to cut deep into the truth; brace yourself.

Good thing the mirror only shows an outward reflection.
That's not you and you wouldn't want to see you in many cases.
Once you see yourself as is, you'll probably not like the truth.
For truth is always comfortable to accept when it's complimentary
But when truth invades your privacy and shows your flaws, fingers get pointed.

Many would prefer to hear a complimentary lie; than the ugly revealing truth.
Excuses and justifications become the temporary exit, not what most like to read about.
Wrapped up in a world of can't do's and self-appointed limitations
The light of restriction never overwhelms the darkness of submission.
Now that cuts deep and the rest prefer it to go right over their head, confused?
Walking in the night, convincing themselves their light makes it day.

I saw a man walk in strength, that most by today's standards, saw it as weakness
Many not realizing the easy way out requires little or no discipline.
For yes, even you can appreciate the rewards of hard work, craving a pat on your back?
But spending so much good energy on ways to avoid what brings a smile.
Maybe I'll just scratch my head and brainstorm because I refuse to go out like that.

Chapter 22

When casual Matures

For a short period, I watched and listened from afar.
I knew you appealed and might be good for me?
I casually approached you with an extended hand.
I could tell by your interactions with others
That our similarities would make us good comrades.

Of course, that was only a view outside your private life.
As we continued to chat, I saw some of your defensive chains break.
At first, what was casual had now turned into a hook, extending for your heart.
In time, we appreciated hearing from each other regularly, almost a personal
cure-all.

We craved each other's wit, challenging and motivating us to ascend.
We craved each other's humor, inciting us to live above the daily hassles and crises.
This grew into a larger concern for each other's wellbeing.
This grew into an adult admiration that generated blossoming.
Like neither of us would have ever expected, more broken chains.

On days I wouldn't hear from him made the reconvening magnify
As to the validity of this invasion, I questioned myself, as walls crumbled?
Daily I questioned myself, or was I fighting answers to my own prayers?
But was it fair and was it right, and why can't I accept what is good for me?

On days where we communicated, by whatever means
Seems to always turn out for all good, even a seldom dispute.
My soul was becoming more addicted, realizing my own maturation.
My mind was becoming more enthralled by his resourcefulness.

My autonomy wouldn't allow me to become dependent as per a crutch in a crunch.
I attempted to pull away on occasions but realized that was more painful.
But it always seemed as if some mishap would persuade to resume,
To your presence of calming and enjoyment, just to mention a few benefits.
Most resolutions just won't come through with such clarity and timelyness.

Even when I tried to rationalize it all out
His words of enlightenment bring a more appropriate ease
But now my heart is convinced by my overbearing mind
As I labored in heartfelt anguish to accept the mental sharpening, knowing
It's truly better to adore and lose than not to ever have adored?

Chapter 23

Zombie Driving

In the process of finding your way
You'll run into some frustration and stress, a plenty.
Displaced anger and suppressed affections,
Leaders emulating followers in inept positions
Gold spooners with their road paved, taking the gravel road to impress.

The growing pangs of loneliness in personal maturation or run,
Severing the superseding pleasures that erode daily irritations
Don't you just love to stupefy the maxims?
Channeling energies to avoid your true pathway
Let me slow down, so you can catch your breath!

Lost in the profession, lost in the game
Lost in others, lost in the shallows, or just hiding
Too timid to escape their own worst enemy
Too passive to appreciate their own opulence
Zombies driving from the back seat.

Hear the chimes and hear the alarm sound off
As new opportunities of awakening are before you
As new challenges that will provide an escape from your nightmares
Where your unfortunate past will no longer haunt you, nor rule
Release from your fears and the overwhelming guild bondage.

Your sands of time are about to expire in your procrastination.
As you assess yourself, your integrity, and your dissatisfactions
Learning to trust your own new persuasions in what defines you
While Zombies drive from the back seat, don't flounder now?
There are way too many ungrateful zombies driving.
Who's driving this bus, the Zombies.

Chapter 24

The Bounty on your head

I can appreciate your cavalier efforts to do what's right.
You made a stand when others only cower; the weak may ridicule you.
You expressed what most were too timid to; the weak only second guessed you.
You faced your fears and theirs also, with a straight back.
, we all know the pay stinks.

In a day when sellouts have no mirrors, just pointing fingers
And the honest, diligent workers get supplanted by the next of kin
When cavaliers survive on pessimism and cynicism
Definitely a diet for the never accountable deceived
As their perceived light shines only outwardly but distorted unbeknownst.

Many now tend to travel from obscurity to a new obscurity
Having minimal light and far less knowledge
Casually trekking through their day without a care, outside their world.
Strictly focused on their essentials, hoping for some icing.
So why give consideration to the depth outside self-regards?

Narcissism spreads fast and is more prevalent than Covid,
Been driven far too much by shallow influences
Been driven far too much by emotionalism
The lost expense to get back to that flash in a pan apex
While most days revolve in a taken-for-granted state of mind.

So, should you allow their voice to belittle your integrity?
Or their opinion to degrade or dictate how you exist
But then again, it can't, if your self-awareness has nascent
Especially if your minds exit ear is open
One of these times, they'll depart in disgust and come to experience
The inevitable depths of life's fragility; look at your watch, now.

CHAPTER 25

JUST STEP ASIDE

Even in my sleep, even in my nightmares
I saw great opportunities.
I saw all the obstacles.
I saw all the challenges as a Win.

Scared of the dark
Scared of the unknown
Scared of the Limits, others inflict
But I can do this, step aside.

The voice won't let me rest
And that's a Good thing
But this pace exceeds all
All that you could withstand, and then some.

Times when motivation applies its brakes
Times when no one can muster any encouragement
Times when everyone doubts
Times when the light just won't shine.

M. A. GRAYSON

I cried as I walked into the fire
Not because of the afflicted heat
No, that won't make me even sweat.
But more so for the heat of affliction.

But believe me!
Yes, and oh, most do now.
Relax on yourself, even in your comfort.
I will do this!
Just step aside.

Chapter 26

Jaded, Never

Taken in as an abandoned pup,
Cold, hungry, wet, and shaking on a chilly winter morn.
No name, no identity and nowhere to lay my head.
I was fortunate to be rescued by the care of a warm heart.

So, she wraps me in a soft blanket
Wisk me off to her humble abode and nourished me.
Now my days have been transformed to good
And my being reformed to reciprocating the same.

I find it a privilege to bask in the sweet of the vine
A place, a life of pleasantries and unsolicited care.
I rest, I wake and I rest again, knowing tomorrow will be even better
Another day to witness the good of a caring heart.

But no one told me a storm was brewing
But I had weathered the storm before, for a small season
Looking death in the face, with starvation strangling me
That caring heart came and rescued me.

But this storm took that heart away
Again, I was abandoned, left to fend for myself
But now I had gained some strength to weather the wilds
Even though my youth limited me to the knowledge of survival.

Even in my daily existence, I struggled to comprehend
Where my caring heart disappeared to and why now?
Was this a part of some diabolical plan?
Was there a fit for me and how would I find it in my youth, place, and value?

So, I wandered and struggled, fighting off death with its various grips
The physical, emotional and mental, always unexpected?
In my youth, not realizing maturation was often the result of overcoming adversity.
The victories in tolerating and enduring those pains?

Every time I would see a resemblance of that heart
It would only be an interior illusion of an exterior resemblance?
But yet I continued, yes, I paced myself, knowing and carefully on watch.
In expectation of a caring heart with my best interest like before.

Yes, in my seclusion, a place I found to reside, or was it hide?
My source of shelter, security, even as uncomfortable as it would be to most
Served its purpose, usually allowing me to protect others from me, now
For who else was left to serve and protect, that expected, seldom experience.

mTg/8/07 ©

CHAPTER 27

BROADER SHOULDERS

The appointed task was extremely burdensome
The requirements and details, so technical
But I, as usual, was up for the challenge.
Yet, again, this put me out on a limb with minimal resources.
So, my boss, knowing this, called with concern for my well-being, for his sake.

That afternoon, a message of wanted consoling a parent on his deathbed came.
That evening, a message about the death of an old friend arrived.
The boss's concern, those messages triggered my extension.
Good friends and family come few and far between
The weeding process is a poem for another book.
But in their dismissal, we reminisce of their touch, their edifications.

Relief comes in so many fashions, or should I say goes?
Words carry so much weight, to say the least.
Even though we've grown so accustomed to preferring visual confirmation.
If we don't let jaded and cynical steal our giddy moments in the sun
Just when you thought they were your best friends because they lessen your risk.

M. A. GRAYSON

The stroke of my pen writes in sincerity, not in ink.
The stroke of my pen writes in blood; it cuts so deep.
From the stroke of my heart, I write of your pain.
From the stroke of my soul, I write of your tears.
Oh, the power of words can console in more ways than we know.

The affection offered is generally more about the mandate received.
Tears and pain are so universal, even if masked, displaced even?
Joy and happiness are universal, too but often welcomed in measure.
Too much of a good thing tends to precipitate complacency.

The challenges can be many, for us that resolve
Whether they're our own or not in sight
Some of us carry the weights, most others share
And the success of the victory can hinge on the previous completions.
Maybe we need to get those wrapped up.
Maybe I need to rely on old faithful, broader shoulders again.

CHAPTER 28

DID THE SUIT FOOL YOU

A fool walks in the dark without a light
Speaks of matters with third-hand knowledge, at best
Defying the motto, two heads are better than one.
Seldom thinking an idea through to the end,
As he directs many to where he's never been.

Have you ever listened to a fool?
Do fools ever listen to themselves?
Not realizing nonsense is knowledge, tried and failed.
While their cohorts just nod and crown them,
Relaying untimely and, therefore, useless knowledge.

Mouth muscles are stronger than the mind
Mind speaking beyond its comprehension
Comprehension extended past its experiences
Ending up lost in their stereotypical paranoia box.
Unable to separate good from useless.

Often driven by pride and self-worth gains
A once in a blue moon good response
Pumps them up to express outside their box
A box lacking observance, just two-year-old wit.

M. A. GRAYSON

Sad thing is they usually stand in failure
Talk with confidence and go almost nowhere
Straddling the fence of existence, unless carried to the next level
Having no wisdom to improvise or modify
Outside their tiny box filled with excuses.

Scared to grow and afraid to go, seeing a change is mandatory.
As they bask in the warmth of complacency.
Is it my title, or did the suit fool you?

CHAPTER 29

EVEN PAIN HAS ITS REWARDS

Another weekend night where you sit all alone.
That might not be so bad, if you had little to offer.
But for you to be so gifted, healthy, and clean,
Yet you chose to take the high road a long time ago.
Most can't endure that emotional pain without some vise or withdrawals.

There has to be something to say for those that:
Won't settle for second best!
Won't succumb to peer and family pressures!
Won't succumb to the concepts that stereotypes inflict!

The priority chain, not to mention your integrity,
Dictated you value your principles and yourself.
Dictated, you thoroughly consider your options wisely.
Dictated that you separate yourself from the norm to excel,
Especially when history has revealed so much in ashes.

As I glance into your life, I noticed,
Yes, you have defied the odds: accepted talk is cheap without enforcement.
You've excelled past the limitations others have set for you.
When one looks inside your life, they see no walls or ceiling.
Who can hold you back but you? Squash the excuses, huh?

M. A. GRAYSON

In your youth, despite the doubters and the can't do cheers,
You've daily swum your way upstream, often alone.
Did all that often, without any encouragement, enduring the chains.
When it would have been so easy to relish over to average success.
No, you had to push the bar beyond what their minds could conceive.

Let others settle for the mundane and be happy in mediocrity.
If you can't be the best and have reciprocity accordingly,
We will let you enjoy your solitude in peace,
Because your sacrifices of being alone have brought value to your integrity.
Sounds like a trip most have chosen to do without, knowing
Pain tolerance is low when your focus isn't peaked on progression.

CHAPTER 30

INTENT, NOT REFLECTIONS

I guess now I can say, with every sunset
I devour more knowledge but have much more to digest.
Even better, coupled with experience, is wisdom that excels.
With that being said, where are you right now?
More importantly, where are you going and what to do?

We all speak our own language, often a mix of variety.
The things we see and taste have our personal receptive stamp.
Whether influenced by our guardians, upbringing, or disciplines
Often by the lack thereof that drives our opinions.

To express a phrase is one concern,
But to expect that same phrase to be interpreted as expressed is a reach.
To be frank, it's more than a reach.
This reach kills most and the relationships they have or are developing.
You may want to read that chorus line again to digest it thoroughly.

I've seen the appreciated gifts go to the trash.
I've witnessed good intentions be misunderstood to the max.
You've been hurt by the right expressions, misworded approach
Then come to find out, if given a chance to rephrase it,
It was expressed right for the giver, but not for the gift.

So, a wrong phrase can be as bad as no phrase at all.
Both have been misinterpreted more than you can count.
Both have been taken as ill when they were meant for betterment.
Guess that's where time spent hearing a heart overcomes the raspy voice.
No matter how delightful it may be presented and the time of night.

Heart ears just aren't used enough!
The ideal words spoken in silence have so much value
But too many rehearsed can be better shown, true intent
With that being said, the heart smile is more urgent than not reflected.

Chapter 31

Another Sad story

A six-year-old boy whisked away from the loving, nurturing arms of his mom
The reaper paid an untimely visit which displaced him to be raised in depression
He found more adoration on the street corner where his craft was enhanced
As his heart made a turn for the worse, the birth of another thug?
But he survived the heat of the streets, but his existence was day to day, at best.

He found the encouragement to at least accept bigger challenges
One that challenged his mind, not just his manhood
This challenge, as temporal as it was, kept him occupied for a moment, new direction
But it still left him without that constant loving care he saw as an infant; such is life?
Not a one attended to his daily needs since that dark day and whoever truly loved him.

Then out of the blue, he stumbled onto a wounded tender heart.
But he only saw the wound; he only saw the need, not the hidden compassion.
He had lived a life full of hurt and pain from wounds, so he knew how to attend to hers
Not realizing that her wounds were far greater than what he could see and there were more.
In time he would gather that, remain to attempt to remedy and appeal to her neglect.

In the midst of his doctoring and with the time it took, she noticed his old wounds
She inadvertently started to attend to his needs out of reciprocity but ever so
cautiously
In time they grew close, sharing their deepest secrets, growing in oblivion
To the extent of gradually neglecting their other interest and cronies, all in
rhapsody
They were being blindsided by love, making each other's day even in the midst of a
storm.
Finally, good stability had become the norm for each of them, hope came true.

In time they saw the light, but that's when their recall of old wounds raised its head
Coupled with nightmares of the past and residual remembrance of abuse
The questions, the doubts and seldom patience in trying to be understood
Rather than empathize, even though they had traveled parallel troubled roads
They would at times retreat into their old internal closure and means of
protection.

Not realizing the pain it would inflict on the other, that really cared
Bleeding at the heart with uncontrollable tears in flow, true love overwhelmed
They parted ways, lost in each other's love, at her request, his words echoing
"You'll miss me when I'm gone" but too stubborn to accept their own dream come
true.
But she reconsidered, realizing in time how much he meant to her and went
for him.
By now, he had gone back to the corner adoration, knowing he couldn't keep her?
Again, the reaper paid an untimely visit and raised enough doubt in her to displace
him.

CHAPTER 32

EMBRACE YOURSELF

Despite how much you prefer to reside in comfort,
Despite how often you get to enjoy the good life,
We all need to visit our own depths periodically, but many refuse.
Taking a little time exploring our dark side, refresh yourself,
All to comprehend where we've been and take inventory of who you are.

Extreme is an outside venture for those that prefer justification.
Here's your chance to quietly release from your personal and hidden undesirables.
Here's also a chance for you to move to the next writing.
Acknowledgment, let alone expressions, of the deep, can be painful.
So, remembrance of the upcoming benefits must remain at the forefront.

Some people on some days bring out the ugly in you.
You allow these people to gain control over you, and it's never pretty.
Why succumb to negativism subject to a moot point?
Then, being perfectly honest, much of the blame needs to be self-applied.
Of course, those closest to you have an inside track emotionally.

Putting all personal care and concerns to the side, including loved ones,
We daily see the ugly dispositions of others and turn up our noses,
But seldom see it in ourselves when we act in a like manner, set on a soak cycle.
Maybe requesting an attitude adjustment makeover is in order,
Add to that a concerted effort to apologize with any inkling of offense.

Sensitivity in reception can be challenging.
Sensitivity given is encouragingly reaped; think twice on that.
But if you desire to remain on the receiving end, time you swallow your pride.
For when being right is more important than peace, often making for an ugly liability?
Embracing yourself for a change of culture might help.

CHAPTER 33

ARE YOU STILL HERE?

Been discounted by some of the worse, critics included
Been educated by some of the best, motivated in my youth
Been hurt, disrespected, and disenfranchised, something you've tasted?
Acceptance has eluded me, thankfully at least at that expense
And under-appreciation has rampantly tried to devour me.

So, I now run my own race even if it's without victory, no fanfare either
I fight for what I believe is right anonymously
I've dined with kings and shook the hands of generals
Have learned more from my death than from living.
Resuscitated life when all others gave up or wouldn't consider it.

Fortunate to be heard without a voice or blame the infected ear
Still, many days I've had to restrain the beast in me.
Have taught more in silence than with a pen
Been called a friend, yet never welcomed
All exercised to bring a sense of relief, different from the demand.

The acquaintances gather at the cemetery
Yes, it's my time to enter the grave, again......Again?
An occasional place of visitation for me
Death has come to also throw dirt in my face, a final time
But that has been done numerous times before.

Just another meaningless death, to most
Caused by another meaningless act of violence.
Would that make it meaningless to the victim or the killer?
Assumptions in death wither when the truth's revealed.
The magnitude of death's lesson when endure, open-mindedly.

CHAPTER 34

BLINDLY EVOLVE

Really English is the hardest language to learn, ever-changing
But we evolve in time, so why not what we express
Speaking like phrases, relaying unlike sentiments
Getting frustrated because we can't be understood, saying the same
So, we sit in disgust, wondering when will we ever be seen as we are?

Many can't even accept true love from another, desiring what's offered
Many can't even realize when true love is presented, translational cataracts
Many can't come to grips that love given to them
Is often the history of love received with gratitude?
So, we're blinded by our own expectations, seldom articulated.

Bemuse me with your definition
Watch me addle you by clarifying the same?
Thus, much concern, much comprehension is lost in the blender
Severing what's staunch with variant expressions of a tantamount.
Somebody better be patient or put their coat on in departure.

Either we exercise our listening abilities, not just hearing
Knowing mercy doesn't start and end with us on our terms
Even though you think second chances end and start with you
Until you trip and require a helping hand more times than offered
So, you continue to walk in alienation, even when you're not aware.

Alienation because who you are or who you aren't
Because of who you refuse to be like, they will try to persuade you
Because you can improvise and make the call, even if isolation is the result.
Because you defy being someone else, regardless of the outcome
Because you know exactly who you are and where that puts you, painfully even.

This is where the true heart lies; because now you lose those in your circle
Now you look bad where many won't be able to comprehend your distancing
Now you feel alienated without true care and less funding
Now you know you define evolution, as words just cloud up matters.

CHAPTER 35

DOUBLE VISION

The potential is living beyond the scope of the dream.
Gravitating, maybe more like repelling what seems easy.
The reality is following and accepting the doubters' fate.
Gravitating towards my comfort zone usually?
The thin line of separation hinged on choice, I mean persistence.

It's often as simple as will I sit or will I stand.
Will I walk, or will I ride in the back seat again?
Will I be assertive in concurring with the crowd or defy their beckoning call?
Will I follow my convictions or be a part of the group, identified by number?
I'm starting to see double already.

So many decisions in so many directions with so many possible outcomes.
It's ironic how we come to so many different conclusions without moving.
Often either comfort at the beginning leading to struggles in the end,
Or complex in the initial developing stages and enjoy the pleasures later.
While most fall for the illusion of permanent comfort, which results in permanent misery.

In time some fathom hard work brings big rewards, hopefully during a senior
moment.
Others mock that concept, unsuccessfully hoping for the winning roll of the dice.
Sadly, a few wait for the drop of a lucrative insurance policy or lotto ticket.
Seldom having the wherewithal to capitalize or preserve such a lofty windfall.
While the remnant daily perch on greeter's bench venting outside their knowledge.

Appreciating the voice of the wise in dead silence.
Appreciating the voice of the dead in wise motivation.
Does the choice make the result any more vivid?
Or do the results make the choice more vivid?
Double vision makes you question your next move.

CHAPTER 36

DIRTY FACE

Do you have a clue to all the areas where unjust decisions are made on your behalf?
Many tarnishing a good legacy by the silence of revealing truths behind closed doors,
Rescuing many, knowing when to have an open mind & when to turn a deaf ear.
Do you even care what comments determine a stop or acceptance allowed in your life?

Whether it's your appearance, how you carry yourself, or how you smell,
Whether it's your gait, your beliefs, or your choice in a music genre
And just to think, Dirty Face was my uncle's beautiful cat that looked like it had a facial smudge
A smudge that goes beyond appearance, accent, or cultural differences.

Even as others that have separated themselves from you without offering you an honest chance
Excluded from the group, forbad from a promotion, or proscribed from merging
Because they feel threatened, afraid to be ostracized by association, or that you may outperform them?
Not something they'd ever attest to, yet a benefit you may grow from, enduring the haunting pain.

Disregarding & discrediting, knowing unspoken thwarted expectations can birth disappointment

Not realizing their morals are blended with a core of hate & self-absorption

Then again, how many times have they mentioned those kinds of people?

Where inclusion & diversity is a debate, they distance themselves since it doesn't benefit them.

This may knock your socks off, but there are barriers put up, so you'll never advance, unspoken rule!

Achievements you'll never conquer, not while I'm in charge mindset, despite your credentials!

So please don't fool yourself to think, it's all about how well you perform, consider your audience?

Nothing personal, but you're not qualified, overqualified, or just not a good fit in some places.

Sand thrown in your gears to discourage test your character & can also mature you in right choices.

In spite of your smudge, realize decisions are made for you to be a house cat, barn cat, or street cat.

CHAPTER 37

RETHINK THAT, BEFORE YOU

It reverberates in my mind flooding my heart with the daily.
It may resonate mentally but gets filtered out in exchange for the wasteful.
How have we shut ourselves off to all their pains and needs?
How have we allowed ourselves to get so caught up in the frivolous?
How have we become blinded to the essentials of others, and for what?

When will I learn my vent is so insignificant compared to listening?
When will I learn age should match up with some degree of maturation?
Every day, we see it in all the wars of the mind resulting in mind wars.
We can try to hide in that, glad it wasn't me or another guy syndrome.
But if it gets to you, then you'll be stuck in that, why me syndrome.

Please, pain is universal and a respecter of no one, if you haven't tasted it yet?
Some tolerate it better than others and some have to endure more
The same goes for the struggles, ethics, politics and so on,
We all come from a dysfunctional family, but if it makes you feel better, swallow
For the sake of a book or look, many think there is a perfect home.
Just because it looks better than yours or the people act civilized, cosmetics sell.

Our theories and remedies all need therapy, not to mention some of the things
you read
Blame the writers or the proofreader, maybe even a newscaster or a politician.
Throw in a few columnists, a twisted evangelical and several lawyers, because
you know
That was picking the low-hanging fruit, knowing you can drown being
overwhelmed?
Give some men a title, an office and a mahogany desk and his judgment goes to
kerplunk.

For a season, we attempt to progress without much troubles
Then the next season, it may get worse or better, or maybe I can win the lotto
Self-preservation ruling varies immensely according to the varying self
Tolerate and dismissal or struggle and survive goes to the fittest
Now you see why road rage has become a daily concern.
Just when you thought that was an accident?

CHAPTER 38

WORDS CAN'T EXPRESS
EVERYTHING

I know my day in the sun will come, but I recognize that's not the point.
Energy spent, for Pete's sake, of course, the line doesn't end with him.
But enough with the pleasantries, you want to get to the depth of your crisis
Energies spent, under-appreciated because the focus remains on the half-empty glass.
Makes one wonder if the effort is worth it, but that's not what drives me, so I press on.

Look at the struggle of the homeless as he pushes away his concerns in a cart
See the seared hearts of some of the prosperous, ascending without concern for who
They travel the same roads, yet only one exists as the other becomes a fixture
Trying to get ahead, by any means necessary and yet neglecting their beginning
All a part of the continuing saga of another senseless tragedy.

They call your name looking for an opportunity to release their frustrations on you
They call your name hoping your fall, no thanks to their push, will encourage their rise
They search for you, hoping that if they can't ascend, they'll work to hold you back too.
They belittle your accomplishments because they have no trophies to show.
They live in a self-absorbed dark closet, calling it home.

The subtle darts are thrown to discourage or bring you down below their level
Living in glass houses, so what's their point in throwing rocks?
Can all rise above the hidden words of degradation?
Can all stand in the fire of discouragement and still find the gumption to proceed.
I don't know about all, but you can...time to stand.

Much said with encouraging intention often results in discouragement due to presentation
Much said with enlightening intention often results in misdirection because of self-doubt.
What I meant was maybe I assume too much because I just never took the time to ask
What I meant would have had a more effective influence if I had only listened, first
Now there's a new concept, listen more attentively?

Is that like listening minus the shoulder chip, maybe a preconceived plot?
Trying to understand another's view, even if I know it differs from mine
Or must I convert everyone and only believe the ones that have like ideas are gold?
Then again, education is often only as valid as its source!
Then again, words can't express everything; some things have to be witnessed.
Then again, unconditional love portrays more than mere words can relay.

CHAPTER 39

YOU DENY YOURSELF

Til death do we part, they say, when most prefer to follow the easy paths?
As we travel on treacherous roads surrounded by pathetic drivers.
They show what they want you to see within the confinements of defense
The same walls that repel what's bad repel good in poor oversight.
But the heart will tell all in time if you'll just learn how to listen.

Unbidden opportunities try to devour in the cross hairs of a hope scope
Yet, those generally aren't the same as the sought out ones.
So much of a day spent on discarding the influxes.
Which leaves very little to enhance what's appropriate
Even though the interest wanes in an overwhelming course, the big picture.

Most go to countless ends to hear the truth, comforts in spinning it
But accept it at their convenience and prefer it seasoned without accountability.
Accepting their personal revelation seems so insurmountable
Many just can't handle that much truth, spoon-feed me.
Is it time for Happy Hour yet?

Your attributes can't always be comprehended by those with the same.
Of course, less by those without, even if you give them a clue.
Pain and discouragement is often expressed in defensiveness; learn to listen quietly
While joy and encouragement is expressed in offense, respond with gratitude.
Frustration is expressed due to the imbalance of those leaning in favor of
misfortunes.

If you know yourself, then you also know your needs and frailties.
Some preference is vain and others can be of necessity.
Some preference is lost in self-regard, others in objectivity.
Some preference is about loss, others in the history of what was lost.
But don't deny yourself the satisfaction of accepting; life is bigger than me.

CHAPTER 40

YOUR CLOUDED VIEW

Is it too much to ask and I know you have
Defying the theories, denying publications that define women
Elaborating on how to communicate and understand them
Denying the articles and defying the leads about men
That would depict their traits, confining them to a box,
Piquing your curiosity by riding the high ground of literature is obvious.

Comprehending at the sake of suppressing their growth and individuality
We despise that in reception; yet serve it daily on a stereotypical platter
Transmitting what we care not to accept, or maybe that's a poor example
Craving the advantages, but not the advance according to your watch.
Satisfied in the completion, yet we seek a greater aspiration.

Emotions driven with passion a fire without smoke and mirrors
Abstrusely absorbing the technicalities via emotions
Delegating the compassion driven task via a formal procedure
Negating the gray areas and wishing dismissal of the thin line betwixt
Perceiving what's not being said when nothing is expressed.

Assumptions of silence, assumptions of the seldom-heard
Haven't you ever asked yourself, why do others characterize me like that?
In a far different light than what you see of yourself, some good and some you wonder
How in my weakness few see my strengths, now cling.
In my failures, or what appears to me that way, they see progress.
Some even in your victor will see failure: see your exit.

A clean mirror still shows merely a decent reflection,
As painful as it has been in serving, I'll keep my glasses clean to see objectively
What I see in you far beyond your view and hear what you've miss
For the further, the object is from your eyes or in most cases, the less seen
Clarity for you is lessened but for me made unclouded.
Where can you be valued per your own merit?

CHAPTER 41

HOPE AND PRAY

Simply amazing how you're seen when you don't want to be
Not noticing when you feel the need and prep for the lights
Then again, the cynical voice gets louder with age, not wisdom.
So, let's visit the real world, especially the undisclosed side.
Maybe a personal revelation can awaken you, or at least enlighten.

Most nowadays admire advanced book knowledge acquired with time, a degree.
Many also admire the street common sense when it's versed or put to appropriate use.
But watch the voices quiet when the wise enter the room, as they stare attentively.
Bringing clarity to your dilemma and resolving what the book and country idioms couldn't
You want that association and to have that person on speed dial.

Admiration from afar can be a good thing, recognizing that person's eccentricity.
Even in the midst of what you need, you doubt not expecting, but go through the motions.
Yet the old wise one comes through, even as you fight against yourself
Daily fighting against your own goals, even those you love the most and pray for
Contradicting the very lessons you teach and disciplines you try to instill.

Desiring to hear the truth and wanting to see your true self, feelings aside?
Yet when that picture appears, you laugh and point fingers in total denial.
Walk away from your opportunity for progress in exchange for a recliner in a ditch
Stuck in the ditch, lost in the shuffle, you get carted off acknowledged by a number.
All the cosmetics and beautician help in the world couldn't revive your identity.

Lost in an amorphous emotional state of mind, yet you passionately let it guide you
Preferred over the confinements of the rational to save face, at least look good?
Pondering the dismantling of success at the expense of predetermination
Recognizing true enough interest shown in the pursuit of success
Far outweighs the norm of worrying in distress of the same.

Just another callous mindset of unnecessarily laboring because you limit others
Not just physically, but also mentally, psychologically and emotionally.
Yet you promise the chains of your ancestry still have a voice that you've allowed
The winds sound off in a chorus of freedom and relief to those that will vacate solace
To those that refuse to stay lost in the shuffle, run for your life and for those that listen.

CHAPTER 42

MISUNDERSTOOD

So preoccupied with my response and how I would handle the matter.
So preoccupied with what works so well for me, seeing my success.
She almost unintentionally walked into her own fate, yet hers isn't mine.
Declination of foul selections recognition and disgust drove her
Yet, she would awaken in time to see daylight.

What ever happened to the days when girls grew up to be ladies?
The days when men handled their responsibilities no matter the expense.
The days when a handshake and your word were bond.
Is it cunning, indecisive, or just inconsiderate that has allowed this demise?
Seeing evolution isn't as progressive, or is history not repeating itself.

Shifting gears, for even a man under duress will leak an occasional tear
So, they do have emotions, even though it's shown differently than hers
And since that's the case, she goes right through the signs into distrust
Such a heavy price to pay for poor recognition, but ignorance is blinding.
And their commitment was binding, however vague the comprehension.

His silence and vacancy said the same as her frustrations vocalized.
They were on the same page and never realized it.
Their concerns were identical, yet they thought they were so different
They argued daily in agreement, but stubbornness covered their sight of it.
It's infectious to both, to all and drives all your closest kin away, despite.

So as the clock continued to tick away their birthdays
Prospering and progress is consumed in a taken for granted nightfall
From the beginning, they were believers and supporters of each other
The seldom-seen guffaws seldom reflect consideration for the other
Words, no matter how often spoken, yet lack consideration, misunderstood.

Take note and make memory for perception of nontransparent hearts emissions
His is misread and hers misinterpreted for all emotional purposes.
Yet the rekindling can be recouped in undivided concern
But for most, that sacrifice is a stretch for the other to make
Following the same suit with the kids, all just misunderstood.

CHAPTER 43

MYSTIFYING TOUGH LOVE

Some call it being mean, as others see it for what it is.
The truth is a hard pill to swallow at the expense of comfort.
We can see the depths of others, yet we miss our own vision.
We can glean the hearts of another without being aware of our faults.
Mine are small to me if I have any, but yours need immediate attention!

Some call it being distant, as others ponder how he can survive?
With the truth devouring their very souls, they walk with conviction.
With the truth devouring their very heart, they walk in freedom.
The games we play with ourselves where we can't see the forest, lost in the trees.
Yet we ask, what will it take to wake my sleeping giant?

We tried to blame others by making them think it was really their fault.
As the truth in us fought off what we knew was our own choice.
The advances and accomplishments just weren't fulfilling,
As we tried to live vicariously in driving them to perfection, as we saw it.
Yet we never tasted the sweetness of that maturated vine.

Some call it being cold, as their standards flutter in the wind.
Our reminiscence of our shortfalls carried less weight than others.
Deaf ears turned where we witness only our valiant successes
Where we'd rather not listen to your excuses, now that we can stand
Insensitive, some call it, as others see tough love, easily given.

Some call it being admired, but who has to suffer in all that?
Dying in ignorance solicited over life after temporary frustration
Hate to question ourselves and hate more to hear the answer.
Devaluing others to justify our means.
So, we dust off our trophies that remind us of the value of the kill.

Passing the onus like a relay baton reflects deceptive self-regard, a trip up.
Now let's see who's left standing true, ascend now.
Some call it being honest in giving, while the few left endure the truth.
Rising to witness it can be lonely in the righteous stratum.
Daily many strive, but few reside; maybe that's the issue.
But who wants loneliness when they can have justification, tough love?

CHAPTER 44

REFUSE TO KILL YOUR HOPE

I asked myself and heard you whisper the same with mind wide open
What will it take for me to escape the daily restraints and grow? Yes, learn of me
Those concerns that impede my progress; that distract the very thought of it
The ignominious laws that have devoured without any enforcement
The numbers say it all, but I don't believe you want to be a victim any longer.

This is where talk ends and those that hunger and thirst after doing right stand up.
This is where the amen corner no longer backs you up in chorus, but exercise changes.
It's not enough to just exist, to be, but to recognize that your life has a far greater value.
Knowing we are more vulnerable in the static state of mere existence
Yet a growing mind, the maturing person is tougher to offend, let alone abuse.

So let us step to the higher grown and devalue ourselves no longer, refuting our denial
One of many enemies to our progress, like ignorance and self-deprivation.
Self-awareness gives us the foundational fortitude to repel hatred and rejection
Self-appreciation and self-acceptance is a product of that refined awareness
Awareness via personal knowledge of our pros and cons, developing discipline in that.

M. A. GRAYSON

It all starts with that simple concept of planting fecund seeds in fertile soil
Inclusive of everyone, regardless of upbringing, faith, gender, or amount of tax shelters
Yet we see the prep of the soil is as important as you the seed and your genetic disposition
Here's a time I must give accolades to those dedicated to the tilling of the soil
Usually, small gratifications for such a high demanding and underappreciated endeavor.

Thanks to Mom and even the Mr. Moms for their sacrifices, aunts and uncles too.
Some have arrived and matured to keep an eye on, guide the prize, the true value of a child
Not limiting that child to their dream, but allowing the child to grow into their own
Not confining the child to their knowledge, but allowing that child to ascend beyond that
Advancing that child's self-awareness even in tough love without smothering them.

My appreciation for the same encourages me to release my child to the same knowledge
Encourages me to do likewise for other children, desiring their best, too.
Knowing it will be for our best, allowing their individuality to constructively expand
Allowing their hunger for knowledge to have a progressive direction and be satisfied.
Not allowing limitations to kill their hope, even if ours was.

CHAPTER 45

INSIDE THESE STONE WALLS

Now you see why I seldom smile in appreciation for its value
Minus the children and an occasional friendly greeting.
Maybe to reflect concurrence in a pact, never mind the austere
Maybe to express, all is good in the midst of the battle.
In all seriousness, I stay palpable and sensitive to the concerns.

The tears that never show up in the light and what causes it
Unexpressed pains with confounded daunt
Those that you think have no emotions when hit low unexpectedly
More like those that reveal their emotions differently than you,
Thus, put you in doubt until you're there in their moment.

When fate takes control over your very being, so surreal
Yet, for many, far less will drive them upon awakening.
Yet the driver, the circumstance measures your resolve
So, strength inside these stone walls or even the weaknesses
Is a product of the strength of that same foundation.

So, I can execute what I know to be right, as if you will accept that
Even when it differs from what may not be your best practice
It may be tough for you to comprehend, tougher to put into action
Now that I've grown to understand why silence is golden
Maybe it's because I got another chance to listen.

M. A. GRAYSON

The extensions of love come in a multitude of ways beyond my scope
Determining my very boundaries of resilience
Unveiling what appears to many to be my opaque disposition
And all the time, the obvious was lost in your perception of the assumed.
Silence can be deadly while listening with eye contact so appealing.

So, as I resist the urges, Excuse me if I don't follow the slaughtered.
The necessities lost in the overwhelming fetishes
Inside these stone walls, you hear no chorus, not a single note
With a single eye for overachieving, even if it is your call
That explains why there's little beauty inside these old stone walls.

CHAPTER 46

HISTORY PUT ME IN MY PLACE

They say what doesn't break you makes you stronger!
Daily we break and daily we get stronger.
In that lies the craving for substances and a comfy blanket?
Yet some of us take the low road and endure the undeserving afflictions
Some just won't assume the position.

The easy road is the choice of preference for most
To fight, to throw the books in the court of law
To counteract ugly for hate only breeds more hate?
An ever condescending travel spiraling downward
But to rebut that requires more energy, let alone self-disregard.

What many prefer to fight, I peacefully choose to conquer
Again, that would set one in martyr's row
Comfy creates a world of living oblivious to the life of the struggle
Justifying my gains and what's right, in my view, being important!
Yes, the struggle lives yet today.

Not recognizing the strengths and standards that define you?
Not realizing the personal burdens you bear outside of you?
Better define your climb, even your legacy!
The same that resonates your integrity,
Yet, for many is what that catapults them into derogation.

M. A. GRAYSON

Slowly devoured in a taste of mom's apple pie and her reasoning
Their walk, their voice diminishes in influence
Trying to fit in where they can get in
Fighting for all the wrong reasons, self-regard rules
The temporal and others' opinion vaults to the forefront.

Preferring the fight to prove me right
Over the peace for a numerous maturation
Leaving history to put me in my place.
Is it my time for a stand down, again?

CHAPTER 47

REFRESHING UNTIL THE DEPARTURE

Peeking through the window of old
Walking down the roads of my younger days
Haven't been here for a while as it reminds me of yesteryear
I'm approached by old faces and toxic phrases.
Those would bring smiles, and others would generate frowns.

As the aroma after a cooling summer rain, refreshing
As the freshness of a stick of spearmint gum to quiet the bitter breath
That deep belly laugh brought on by the innocent yet frankness of a child
The comfort of a hot shower after a long hard day of work
Can't omit hearing a timely old tune, refreshing.

The long quiet ride after a passionate, heated argument
An ice-cold beverage on a hot, humid day of excessive labor
A clean bathroom when you're away from home
That good efficient heater after coming in on a very cold day
A hot home-cooked meal after an extended trip.

Basking in the comforts of convenience and familiarity
Yet the opposite often tends to bring more development
Repelling the truth because it just doesn't feel right
Raising a standard against your allies, not in your blood?
Selling your valuable integrity for a tickle, cheapening.

M. A. GRAYSON

The extent of the efforts made to bring satisfaction going unnoticed
But the self-regard eyes weren't raised that way
Even givers were just that on a beautiful day
So, I park, as I see the defense taking the steering wheel
The blinding expectations blur the view in the choice to give up on you.

So, you're left with the forever question
What brought this on because you were stuck on you?
Now push rewind and see what's really refreshing.
Or push play and see what's really evolving.

Chapter 48

Best of a Short Visit

Termination notice – that unexpected time of year discharge
Reverberating the imparted love, developmental installments
Unfamiliar boundaries of tolerance seldom witnessed
Remembrance of expressions of strength, if not a coy decoy
When in reality, it was a final gasp for mere existence.

Stumbling over a small crack in the road
Choking on a small morsel of bread pudding
What builds vigor in one detracts the vitality of another.
Never knowing the whence of your final gesture
How often would we inquire; if I only knew it was our last visit?

Now you know the areas of your strengths, for many never sought
Generally can be the very demise of your journey
Since like mirrors would reflect our differences
By contrast, do the different mirrors reflect our likeness?
Makes you wonder what came first, the person or the purpose?

No confidence, no applause makes for a minimal pursuit
No hunger, no aroma makes for minimal attraction.
The struggles expensed meandering
In the long haul, minimize the depths and value of life itself.
Under-appreciated for lack of success and a revelation.

Influences of the wrong side of the bed decisions
Influences of that call you never initiated
Influences of rejection and disapproval.
Influences of a streak of inconveniences, innuendos and inconsideration?
Let's see how much root those childhood disciplines took now.

Please remind me, everything that happens to me isn't always about me
In self-regard, that can get dismissed because we don't see the big picture
The small picture can exclude us all together, as it rejuvenates life in us
Handling matters and not allowing them to handle us
As we again appreciate the lesson learned in the short term.

CHAPTER 49

WHERE DO I KNOW YOU FROM?

No one hears your cries and few seem to really care until you're on the brink.
Depreciating your altruism, devaluing your painful overextensions
Swollen, supersaturated in their own blank sheet.
As you recall your mom's voice, the hard lessons learned
Even though many weren't devoured without a scar and no need to show them.

Often the matters that are toughest to speak on
Often the matters that are hardest to address
The concerns that are dearest to your heart remain in a quiet darkness
The ones which are difficult to discuss and face, let alone disclose
Are the very same ones that bring maturation, relief when endured with foresight?

Whether they accept you or not, even in your ugly glory!
The different paths you choose along with your subjectivity
From dad's commanding dictations to respecting the difference in others
Why can't you be like your brother and reciprocate the same?
Relative is the day one realizes, your respect for others may differ from your guardians.

For you got the memo, your time is about to expire
That's when you first really woke up to see the true value of the taken for granted
You quickly lost your jaded view with the timepiece
Maybe just dismissed the discouraging influences, as you caressed your own chortle.
As you finally realize pain is yesterday, why invite it to today's schedule.

So, you maintain sanity without balance as you venture into the vacuum of revelations.
As it tries to inhale you in deeper, but you squirm, afraid you're losing your identity
No longer recognized as the same gift that overtakes you in its development
Also, is it making it nearly impossible for you to stay acquainted socially?
The forbidden atmosphere of isolation in cooperation with dream reruns.

Where most vacate you, preferring comfy over misunderstood
Preferring the easy, the familiar over the gravity of excellence with peace
Preferring the ruts and potholes over making their own level roads
All because of lack of approval or someone else's blind influences.
Only makes you wonder, where do I know you from?

CHAPTER 50

NOT EXPEDIENT TODAY

Let's cut to the chase, so brace yourself for the ride
That's right, you won't be driving and lucky if you don't dismount before we stop.
Always being politically correct can equate to riding the fence, as in no backbone.
Distinguishing the absolute truth from your skewed point of view, at what cost?
A land of understanding where most never gravitate towards reality, preferring
denial.

The differences of views, even when objective, tend to sway their audience
Thriving and justifying their stand on the applause of the fence riders.
Rather be right than do what makes for peace, even when wrong
No longer mind over matter descending to the fear over matter abyss
Where truth is cheaper than fabrications and innuendos.
Where it just sounds right, roll off the tongue more fluidly.

So now you've been handed the mic but know, Now's not the time to expound
So now you've been given the opportunity, but know this isn't the right place
Now you've been put in an awkward scenario but realize it's more prudent to listen
You've been spoken ill of, but know you never have to justify your actions
Clarity is often for those void of understanding, even to some that prefer drama.

There's a proper place for things just as there's a proper time for the like
Restraint and discipline are necessities taught as a child, seldom exercised as adults
The power of letters, the influences of words should be enough
Enough to appreciate energizing encouraging words when serving
Become reception of the same, sweet to the taste and brightening of your day.

Sit and listen to the birds as you drift off into a beautiful, peaceful place
Simple truth is those that go to peaceful places usually don't have peace?
Yet the views of you to others and it only reminds you
To fill tomorrow with the same in all your presentations
Or at least do the expedient thing and remain quiet when in the company of the distorted.

Just for the sake of being right, correcting the insignificant
Losing vision of the essential in the transporter.

Chapter 51

I'm Tired and going home

Life is ever so precious, even so much more delicate.
We expect the weak, the feeble to surrender
But I saw death's angel with no respecter of status or affiliation
Sneak up again, for when is a good time for his arrival.
Even many volunteers underestimate life values, the purpose of their journey.

Lost in our neighborhood, in our loved ones
Lost in our jobs, maybe in an inheritance
Lost in the status quo or aspirations of tomorrow
The frailties of mirror tunnel vision
Expense all that effort for what?

Soar high like the eagle in all your heart's desire
And what are you left with at the conclusion?
Reset your goals to accomplish even more, what fire and floods can't devour.
Then there are those that have never had the opportunity to enjoy your mundane life?
They smile daily and love knowing pain is in existence.

Appreciating both the joys and sorrows of yesterday.
Mustering up the strengths that have been afforded them
Preserved for the fulfillment of what the blind man saw
The load can get heavy at times, especially for those that extend beyond their own
That's where you can find rest beyond your own resources.

I'm tired and now it's time to go home
But first, let me complete the task at hand and extend a hand.
Let me first regain focus on the big picture, even bigger than me and my world.
That's quite a bit to comprehend, or are you ready, not afraid of the next world.
I'm tired and going home.

CHAPTER 52

ABANDONED HEART

Traversing on to the next vertex, one near you
Remaining confident, maybe even looking forward to it
Consistent misclassification in describing me as something I'm not
Speckled it with a trace of reality: a lot of speculations with a touch of their history
That has often made extreme assumptions of my capabilities and concerns
Since I'm accountable, I consider my quiet contributions and an occasional foreign truth.

I listened to the voices of those that claim they're dearest to my heart
Those with my personal interest at heart and then some
Early one aurora, after awakening out of my youthful rest
I now could see as a runaway train about to run me over
My senses acutely tuned in to the never yielded.

Objectives became ever so clear and not just about me!
My elders made time to express the missing pieces of yesteryear.
My guardians found relief in relaying the untold pains they experienced.
But should those revelations of what's best for you hamper my pursuit
Or, in the name of peace, be kept under wraps?
Education for many comes only after the bruise, for you'll carry me, no more.

Accommodating almost to a fault
Realizing tomorrow is the step not advanced today
Especially when listening becomes louder than your way of thinking
Stumbling over true love or tripping over real love
Comprehending depth by observing and with intent listening.

Admirable concerns by reciprocating interested parties
Dearest push their own program with little regard for your strengths
No ear, minimal considerations of the differences and less support
Limiting your tomorrow by what they can't see in you
Limiting your today by what they couldn't accomplish.

Expressions of hollow words, yet believing they're imparting advanced knowledge
Ever so close physically, but in-depth clueless
Conventional thinking says the first phase of abandoning is verbal restraint
But conventional wisdom says the first phase is in not listening.
Abandoning their dream by my limitations, by my misnomers.

Chapter 53

Viewing through rose-colored glasses

The experiment was to Look through a classmates glasses
To experience the contrast of like images by a different view
Reflecting, we see others, never the same as they see themselves
Physically and even more so characteristically
So at least consider submitting your RSVP.

My ears devoured the various views of me
From adolescence through today
Yet as I consumed their words and expressions
Personal sentiments, observations, yes, their truths of me
In disbelief, I was surprised to see how they saw me.

Whether potentially or in actuality, good, bad, or indifferent.
Others seldom can comprehend your vision as you do.
By the same token, I know their view couldn't be further from the truth
Here the outcome doesn't justify the means and I know you've been here, too.
But I knew my perception had little place for another skewed mislabeling.

Maybe that's why my considerate perspective remains inclined for your good
Transforming your darkness into a state of titillation
Many see your beginning and many see your today,
Occasionally some partial intermediate activities
Yet that's never enough to quantify your heart, pursuits nor your identity.

M. A. Grayson

In as much clarity it provides, glasses are meant for external purposes
When the far more accurate accessing feature is the least used, the view is skewed
When the far most accurate accessing quality is the least relied on, the view is
overlooked
They're used more for self-preservation
So, in accepting your colored view and often a misconception, I digress.
So please bear with me and I'll try not to return the favor.

CHAPTER 54

IF I DON'T -DESTRUCT

After eons, I've finally recognized my strength
Learned to appreciate the after-effects of my defeats
That doesn't equate to my demise via grace
Especially since the ascension by acquisition
Is dependent on today's application.

Even though I walk the route, the traditional just have forsaken
Being consumed from the inside out
My heart refuses to be swayed by the convictions of others
For I know, I must vouch for my stand, accountability
Again, appreciating the message of the quiet.

In spite of their frustrations which may generate pain
In spite of their lack of compassion and, therefore, passion
I realize my mantra is incomprehensible to the masses
Concluding in some days, you just have to walk alone
Other days you'll be left standing alone, which can be good, too.

When you know, you're in the right place, for you
Definitely, when you know, this isn't their purpose
Just because it's the loudest or the final word
Doesn't make it the correct one or a logical resolution.
Dispelling that melancholy spirit if I don't self-destruct.

CHAPTER 55

DEVALUING FOREIGN FRUSTRATIONS

Casualties of stepping on others, even when unintentional, have to stop!
Getting caught up in the pursuit of what's a personal gain at someone expense
Lost in the tunnel vision of what appears to be advancing
Lost in a distorted concept of compensation for the overdue debts
Many have gone on to rest, as gratitude tried to choke the purpose to death.

Despite the pains it brings and the never understood truth, many have tripped over
Rather continue to stumble in the dark for self-preservation's sake
Then see in the light what are truly their shortfalls?
The comforts fought so hard for to dismiss the pain of growth
Like the enticing topping of a decadent dessert to the eyes of one with a sweet tooth.

The distaste of a true medicinal remedy
Now may be a good time to swallow that lump in your throat
Truth be known, selfishness makes clowns of us all when we submit
Foolishness makes idiots of us when we're driven by its dark forces
And yet we restrain ourselves in giving what we know only brings good
For what good reason as you boast of your strength.

Strength doesn't have to have the last word
Strength doesn't need to be validated
Strength doesn't look for an audience; the audience looks for it.
Strength hears what's never been said and resolves with quickness.
For strength is only as good as the wisdom that positions its bearings.

Yet every day, the jockeying continues, back and forth
No gains and increasing the pains
Weeping in the night and craving for what's right in front of your nose, smell.
Greener grass on your side of the fence is seldom appreciated
Too busy abandoning the bleak truth for frustrations of colorful assumptions.

Frustrated in the inability to control the foreign because of entitlement
But not in controlling the warranted domestic generosities
Yet both want the same, even though expressed differently when echoed.
The displeasure of frustration and its source need be replaced with the simple.

CHAPTER 56

THE CHOSEN DESTINY

It was the only candle burning in that old secluded cold shed
She sat alone again, staring into the clear dark night.
Pondering her loneliness and the road that made this all possible
Predisposed to the mandating of her personal past and principles enforced.
Was this her fate by default or lack of concessions offered?

Her daylight aplomb continued to embrace her ghost in the evening
Making it easy to voice her disdain, but she was cut from a different cloth.
Finding it difficult to voice the masked gratitude, can't become vulnerable again?
Being true to herself, unlike many that prefer to cozen with a kiss of death
Now realizing her strength dictated her destiny.

Wanting the dream fulfilled and expecting the gift
In an ideal time and an unexpected day, probably the unrecognizable diamond in
the rough
When it all finally comes to fruition and appears before her very eyes
The glory becomes unacceptable on account of settling
Cruising in mental laxity as so many have fallen accustomed to.

Followers leading and leaders following just to keep the match even
But she wasn't having that while keeping her focus on that gift
Those that pursue the best empty-handed know effort has to twin knowledge
Absorbing the rejection and even some displaced corrections
She stood strong, affirming, never flinching nor mumbling a word.

Like the lone last leaf on a tree on a windy fall eve
She optimistically maintained her focus despite the dismal forecast
She walked when all odds were against her as well as her closest
Knowing some days, you just have to struggle alone and encourage yourself.
Rather than succumb to the voices of quit and decease from those that never knew hope.

The calling has to mean something in your heart where others can't comprehend
The pain has its integral lessons which cause others to never be able to understand
That difference in why they say, stop, when you know you must proceed
As you reject their suggestions of retreat, knowing the deeper revelation lies ahead
For who knows your heart, what's in your best interest and your destiny?
Yeah, who's better to give that advice without knowing you're chosen?

CHAPTER 57

NAVIGATE

With no one being exempt
Exclusive of the debaters
I discovered the thorn in my side.
Pick your poison, but trust the results; disregard the taste.
As we pinpoint the solution, not just another cosmetically correct answer.

Tied for first, someone chose ego and pride over common sense.
The runner-ups' selected beauty over altruism.
Third place preferred fame to integrity.
Bringing up the rear was fortune choking out genuine concern.
Allowing impressions to make its own vaunting opportunity.

Some things are really difficult to find the appropriate expressions for.
Even more complex to fully perceive as they're presented?
Like understanding an eye to eye message in the dark,
Yet misconstruing pen to paper or words to ear
Perplexing the simple with attention clutter.

Let's get back to the basic dinner table brainstorming.
Abandon the personal frivolity and frolicking for a moment
Because it's starting to get a little too hot, now
But we won't hold you in this very long, promises, promises
Then again, as expected, I guess you'd rather depart now?
Navigate to your nap.

CHAPTER 58

PRICELESS

Relentless, even when fatigue tried to set in and take over
Finding that second gear, that second wind
Without a mentor, a helping hand, or a back scratcher
Not just from its origin and appreciating the nurturing contributions aplenty
Yet this discovery venture called for him to be his own mentor.

I saw two, but one challenge caused me to depart my norm
To see beyond my scope, the adrift theorem
Adore the differences and encourage embracing your dreams
Even that which may seem incomprehensible to others no matter how close
Knowing for every wise man willing to lead, ten thousand need be led
Here is one of those few, still not caught up in admiration.

Many go through life without options, like a diamond in the rough.
Knowing, giving hope provides more options and making aware of the unknown.
Awakening their sight to see their own appreciating values
Maintaining a single-mindedness on their personal development and beyond
Rather than suffocating via wannabe someone's exacerbations.

Unveiling themselves to themselves through conquering resolution
When he wanted me to hold him, I was forbidden
When he thought I wouldn't, I did unbeknownst
He made an easy rise over obstacles as if they were low hurdles
But all along that fortitude resided long before.

Many never saw it coming, nor would they have ever thought
The day would come when they would inquire, where did he come from?
I always knew in time and in magnitude, he would come into his own
Such a beauty to see the seed come to fruition, priceless
More so to see the volumetric gift relay in its season.

CHAPTER 59

LET HIM SLEEP

All answers don't shed light on a subject, often misdirecting.
If every prayer's cry was answered, this wouldn't be a better place?
Just like every ideal isn't original, so goes those that drown daily.
All that are conscious don't necessarily walk in the fullness of daylight.
So goes the norm overflowing with coasters and consumers.

Can we skip the sweet jargon and cleave to a more perfect alteration?
Consumed with a preference for rapacious at a blood sale for benignancy
Quenching the true and valid emotions at the expense of rejection
Suffocating the real and joy at the expense of poisoning overweening ambitions
Being honest in recognizing, while walking in the inclusive dark.

Exclusive and original being left out in the frigid, like an unwanted dog
Struggling to make the call for fear of the heat brought on by idle
Rummaging through the basic course that entangles the legends
Inherited entitlement or assumed by association
Either path is only a figment of a never-explored risk.

Where did the time go exasperated in adrift?
Even more essential, it was lost in nothingness exponentially
The child has an excuse which raises another question in your maturation
Procrastination has become a national defense
Assertive in the big of the small and disregarding the small of the large.

Spoiling your objectives at the expense of their whims
Quieting your demons through artificial accolades
Putting their best foot forward knowing it's just a prosthesis
Accepting favors for favors even from the enemy
A land where the means of progress takes no prisoners.

Walk where it's easy regardless.
Stand where you gain most light despite
Speak beyond knowledge draws bottom feeders.
Panning for loyalty from the avaricious in anticipation that
Friends are those that advance you and scratch your itch.
It's business as usual, as we let him sleep it off.

CHAPTER 60

XENOPHOBIA

He started out with nothing, maybe less than that
Except for a reoccurring dream of flight, but not on a plane.
He never gave it a second thought in his youth
Just going through his daily measures and activities
For the only hope given was the chance to see another day.

Then that strange dream would wake him out of a rainy day of nap
He'd look out the bedroom window, watching lightning crack across the sky
He'd stare into the darkness as if he were seizing the energy it expelled
It consumed him, yet he gathered its magnetism as it made him inimitable
Not realizing the dream was slowly evolving.

Powers and concepts that exceed the mind of the wise, the unexplainable
Those that think they've acquired, excelled
Those that believe they're bigger than life, super today?
Even those that know they deploy the ideal panacea
Then comes that unexpected challenge, baffling question or event, so grounding.

Back to our regularly scheduled task at hand, the dream
Yes, the dream was being sewn into the fabric of his soul
Not just a foreign feature being instilled, also knowledge he couldn't comprehend
But this was him, even though he knew not what was to come
He didn't even take time to figure out its purpose, didn't care.

The flight that would gravitate upwardly, ever so slowly
But also, it could come down just as swiftly with a nod, a simple misstep
Most times, no gesture was required, yet he did have control of it
But the knowledge did reveal one day where this flight would take him
Many inquire of their definition but can't exchange it for their destination.

Most important wasn't about where it would take him
But how he would utilize this to integrate their integral potential
Giving vision to what no others would ever consolidate
Breathing life into what ruthless others prefer to make their daily company
So momentarily step away from the norm for xenophobia's not always bad.

Chapter 61

Just a Shirt

Displaced again, singled out by choice or maybe by destitution
Isolated like a stray slither of slate amongst the sands of the beach
The inquiries raised as to from whence did it come and by what means
Subscribing to what others never comprehend, because they never listened
Abandoned in segregation to wander until cognizance is fulfilled
Or death do you part, the norm.

A reach, a stretch for refinement beyond table nourishments
Just a small display to advance, maybe open their eyes
Just a simple gesture of gracious pardoning beyond one's capability
Just a casual out of the way nod to reverse the misfortune
Just a shirt is all it was, but the interest compounded exponentially.
The means of opening their eyes, the mouth follows and heart to the mind.

Living to give until the gift consumes, then progress is ignorantly lost
The scope becomes narrowed through a comfy pair of slippers and some rest
Overcome by the heat to call it a day, rather than rekindle the forward flame
Rundown by and caught up in the storm of the day
As essence strolls by again, unnoticed
Just like the heal piece of bread left in the bag alone.

M. A. GRAYSON

Reading pages from the wrong book for the task at hand
Condemning right for lack of vision and not being noticed
Cosigning the wrong for the sake of reputation and self-interest
Shaping truth to fit in your shoes at no expense
In all neglecting the greater, the real passion overlooked in
Giving the shirt off your back, knowing it's just a shirt.

CHAPTER 62

QUIETING A GOOD WORD

Need I really say any more?
Some things just need no explanation, except when ignorance holds truth hostage.
In the days of overstating and underestimating, digest slowly
Some prefer to give flowers and others rather a box of candy
But stand or strut strong, bark as loud as you deem to draw attention, squeaky
wheel
Yet they can't find the gumption to speak kindly.

Full of knowledge abroad as they watch home fruit dry up
Got all the answers and know what's best for others
Can't decipher their own simplicities.
Getting lost, caught up in the turbulence of nonsense
Losing perception of what they desire
Forgetting to remember to express gratitude, say grace.

Refusing to be consumed by ugly in all its many facets
Exerting to disallow the death of good
What a concept, being thankful for those unexpected generous influences,
mimicking them
Even at conception, even during the unassuming presentation
Energized you to step upward, hold your head high, quiet apprehensions
Pushed you towards success or insanity?

It's a thin line between the bottom and the best
Daily making rational quality decisions in gravity
Fighting for what's selflessly right
Fighting for what's selfishly complacent
Time to return appreciation to the ones that made me smile today,
By yesteryear's observation or a kind word.

Adapting to express more good than you can inhale
Not waiting until tomorrow, you don't with the sour?
That would quiet another opportunity I may never get again.
Influences beyond the givers' knowledge deserve a say
Quieting that gratitude is thievery.

CHAPTER 63

ONLY BLENDING IN

So, you're going again, where you weren't summoned
Questioning where you are, not to mention who
Actually, where are you, like you'd know, yet dissatisfied
The cancers that erode your very being and felicitous notions
But you need more, need better, alone again?

If you can't be at peace and quietly sleep
Might as well plant a weed-like thought in others
Short timers losing focus on, probably never tasted
Short timers may have never had a legit focus
As the calendar conveys your last days, unbeknownst, waste another?

Refuse to accept the offered second chance, second place too
Never gave the first option a good effort
Because as you are, you're either accepted as is in the here and now
Or maybe they prefer to see the back of your neck in departure
The confident, seemingly obvious vote doesn't equate to the chosen.
Let alone, does it verse the end justifies the means.

May just be a call for less pain and misery, like easy street
Passions, even without emotions, often misinterpret
Either overcompensate or underestimate reality
Truth isn't a crapshoot; just add more fluff
Nor does it need supplements for fulfillment
So, dissatisfaction continues because many can't accept their own.

Now you comprehend why they like the big picture
It maximizes their blending in, as in the isolated can claim immunity
The small picture exemplifies their inefficiencies, do nothing, can't err.
So, their existence is based on excuses, distractions and smoke
Giants in disturbing, but dwarfs in distributing.

Chapter 64

Do I deserve this Pain

This is where you'd love to draw a blank
But it follows you and even wakes you in the dark of night
Many restless bedtimes you toss and turn to force some sleep
You take a tally of what you derive is your shortcomings
Not realizing you've omitted offensives of ignorance, afflicted more pain.

This is where it's not better to give than receive
Only if a high tolerance of pain resides in you and add a cup inverted grace
Many tearful days you lay in contrition
Even though you comprehend it in just being misunderstood
Not realizing you've exchanged fate for faith, self-afflicting more pain.

So, you bring on yourself some pain through attrition, some by favor
It rides you daily, occasionally giving you relief when you're overwhelmed
But in your heart, you know the evidence arises as you slump down in defeat
Crying for reprieve, why me, instead of extending a hand
Time to bake a cake and offer a gift; someone's selling out.

We resend the profound in liberty
Yet prefer the profound in observance, spurning virtues
Calling for in earnest, what's been provided that we take it for granted
Hearing what's never been expressed
While missing what will right us in front of our very heart.

Blinded by pain and deafened by the ugly
Allowing that to overcome all the maturation of strength
Allowing that to overwhelm your heart judgments for defense
As the small disappear, and the smaller never was heard
Especially that which was quietly generated in the daylight.

Many choose to die in the very pains they prepared
Few choose the tougher route, paying the debts and mastering the lessons
The beauty of themselves in the same reflection that repels them
You only deserve the pains you neglect to face in that reflection, is real beauty.

CHAPTER 65

DON'T HATE

What persuades you to excel, ascend and encourage today
Tomorrow in a different setting may be mere words without destiny
The following day in another climate has minimal influence, like who cares?
But in the here, know your power to influence goes beyond your perception
Just because you got to plant a seed doesn't mean you dictate its growth.

Touching you psychologically from a crass point of view
That upcoming event that you looked so forward to
Accepting things you'd rather discard most evenings
Except outside your paradise when your cup is void
Come out of that sheltered closet for at least more than a peek.

One may appreciate your good values and integrity
Your, capacity to give of yourself to many
Not asking for you; at least not all of you
Just share a piece of yourself when it's not so convenient
Where you're not lowering the bar to raise your standard.

Now that's real giving while showing no signs of being distant
Which equates into you having discomfort and displeasure
Just as those that scream that loudest
Means they're in excruciating discomfort, so don't hate!
Maybe it just says they have a lower tolerance?

M. A. Grayson

Maybe it means those that stay out of trouble are idle
Haven't you ever heard something you hated to hear?
Truth be known, you knew it was definitely good for you
Even though it may not have been valid about you
Character adjustments bring growing pangs.

The enduring pains of learning yourself, accepting others' differences
Cause you to progressively do the things you do and say the things you say
Makes you want to retract the things you lack in discipline spilled
Keeps you from expressing what you feel like discouragingly
Knowing being lost should remain in your youth.
Save the drama because there's no room for hate.

CHAPTER 66

BREAKING THROUGH BARRIERS

At times we can be idea overwhelmed, where it's tough to apply it all, even choose.
Times when we can hear, even in the deepest rest, yea, asleep too.
That convincing voice we hear when we know there's a good point to be made
But currently, I have no audience, not an ear, so please listen.
For most of the time, when you're expressing, listening should be the priority.
How much have you learned in talking, yet you exhaust yourself in it, confused?

Falling asleep with inquiries and awaken with solutions
Energized beyond Joe the plumber, too hectic for hospital hours
Seldom satisfied with perfection, knowing 1 day doesn't a lifetime make
But that's my demon to fight for a lifetime
Yet when satisfaction is guaranteed, even achieved
It only adds fuel to my fire, so I must continue on to the next.

That's what generates more perseverance to make another righteous day.
As silence became my anonymous defender, quietness my comfort
But when time or was it your call for peace rang aloud
I could no longer hear myself think
Even in the deepest of rest, I arose.

In spite that many don't want answers and others refuse resolution
Some rather remain in their bed of misery for the company
Surviving off exaggerated and diluted favorable truths
Making their bed in a burning house
Instead of moving on, abandoning, yet rather rehash past blunders.

As the predators look to one upon them, as prey
Forgetting the same hand that pats them on the back
Can also embrace the piercing knife
Their goals having been consumed by gold or its equivalent.
Perishing in fluff as the personal revealed truth appears tomorrow
Because today, I'm just not having it.

CHAPTER 67

FACING THE MUSIC

There's almost never an absolute balance in a relationship.
But in the scheme of it all, give and take can generate amnesty.
In the progressive there's an acquired acceptance of agreeing to disagree.
Recognizing imbalance is often the melting pot of being proactive.
Fear restraining freedoms released in intolerances, holding it hostage.

In it all, she didn't mind taking charge, watch her!
And you'll get no free passes or coupons should you cross her.
Pampering, catering, and obedience are just the beginning of her abilities.
Giving attention to her finer details, some call respect.
Then again, that's just her personal preference to those that see her strengths.

Just because you associate with a winner doesn't make you one?
Just because you associate with a loser won't prematurely schedule your date with
death?
Misguiding leaders and in some cases misdirecting the overconfident followers
happens,
Like that unexpected beat that exacerbates your foul mood
And that pleasant aroma that accelerates your passions.

Expressions that divide and conquer, even to the guarded.
Clichés that attract or at least would draw and embrace your seldom open
emotions.
Yet silence is interpreted in the esteem of the beholder.
Profound news travels slowly, as do the humbling reminders.
So, the incremental gains struggle to bring balance,
As clarity is often clouded by inverted visions and apprehensions.

Chapter 68

Lamentations

Hear the drumbeat rumble smoothly, inviting your foot to adjoin.
Hear the soil cry, hear the soil sing.
Where blood mixes with brow sweat.
Where that flows like a mighty river into open wounds.
From whence your structure and discipline were force-fed.

My great cried so loud, so deep I can hear his lamentations now.
A generational travel of sorts to raise his production level by the crack of a whip.
That whip had one destination and anywhere on his broken body brought submission.
His scars were his medals of honor, influencing persuasion just at the sight of them
Where fear carries a gun and the strong no voice, not even eye contact.

His future, his ambitions were predetermined, but not to his appeal.
For if he can walk, his hands should work regardless of his age or competence.
The callous hands, dirt under his finger, and toenails were enslaved like he
Reflecting just some of the struggles just to exist a truncated life, if that
Endurance just to breathe with no identification, no prowess.

No name, but they called him Mule because of his stature and strength
Restricting him mentally, as if he was one of the beasts of the field
The only living son of Blue and his dad, Big Moe.
The others never made it, thinking they were strong, so voiced
Manhood being judged by conforming and enduring the impression of that whip.

As mothers cried daily, begging to the point of surrendering for their only.
Sacrifices of indiscretion for the indignant and outside the house were no votes.
Displaced justice laid on the back of the innocent
That vicious cycle that you can still mark your calendar today
But in digression, we learn or suffer from the same influences.
So, mind your manners, know your place as you lament internally.

CHAPTER 69

JUST A BAD DAY!

Fly free little bird, as the once again wounded flew toward an open sky
Witnessed by the accrued scars and half-broken feathers
Many unseen scrapes still mentally influenced its flight
Many near-death experiences have redirected its path for the safe, the peaceful
Just like you walk, ride and pursue disappointing your next week in apprehension.

Daily many seek refuge, crave absolution like the bird in their bivouac of choice
For blights and blithe events come in a multitude of ways, at times the same source
Some destined to failure by example, some by excoriation, and others by opportunity
More instinctively by the lack thereof brooding without a view of the sun.
Wondering, can you see them as they make their way overcoming obstacles?

In the midst of an identity crisis, yet no idea they reside on that side of the pendulum
Making changes in their appearance to be seen
Making changes in their appearance to be secure
Feeling the need for attention by any means necessary
Unbeknownst that generally turns the light on for darkness to inscribe.

As they indemnify what they saw from the egg stage, fearful of the predators
Perplexed of the next step, the next flight descending in a spiral, the slow death
Lost, no, caught up in that memory instead of moving on in a dash
Can you hear me as they cry in prayer to be freed?
To see a day full of sunshine and taste the good until their belly's full.

Yet all they want is what you discard
Laughter reflects freedom, even when brief.
They often desire what you complain of, toss away
Never a chance to be decapitated by overindulgence
Never a choice to be embraced without requite, never ever.
And the squeaky wheel thought it had a bad day?

CHAPTER 70

A MUST REREAD

The snowflakes flowed parallel as the wind gave them their direction
Made more visible by the distant dark, barren mountains in the background
As I stared in wonderment as to should I venture into this bad weather?
The things that jump out at you in preparation or in self-preservation
What brings you back safely into that enjoyable reality if you leave?

This is far greater than who's walked in my shoes
So, without being prompted, let me remove myself from the picture
As I fade into the incomprehensible, not a place for the faint of heart
So, you can stay preserved and not have to risk displacing boredom
Most would think, no one really sacrificed the time to know me, let alone interest?

Yea, I was crowned with this gaining insight on crippling levels
But when I get in the zone, most cringe, if they don't run first
Truth is generally good, when accepted in a personal perspective with gain
Contrary to common 3D opinions with upcoming compensation.
Sanity or being misunderstood in complementing the same on the same.

Walking blindly into the dark without stumbling with the mercurial
Even more aware than those that walk in those shoes and environment
Beyond our scope, we try to rationalize, even empathize what we humanly know not
Often expressed in, others can't see what I saw in him or am going through
But to know is to listen to the replays in silence, open-mindedly.

That's about when the snowflakes changed their direction
The same time I figured out the best way to venture into it
As I ponder how important is this trip and for what am I venturing out
When growth has to come with intimidation, a dwarfing cost?
Progressive, profound and proactive.... sounds promising.

CHAPTER 71

BRUISES FROM THE GREAT CONFLICT

It starts early in life, how much did mom and dad discipline, set an example
Feed the condescending appetite and watch it grow to degrade when the heat is
raised
Offering baffling tales of personal applause for those that do philanthropic deeds
Politicking for a stormy day favor with quotes for us
But internally, as long as they don't conflict with his agenda, he claims you.

His team is spelled with I from his heart, except when verbalized in times of peace
How can a parent allow such poison to fester in their beautiful child, Don't they
care?
His vote to integrate is radical until the tide rises against him, when it insults
I hear him sing loud in church and witnessed all the accolades she received in
the same
Offering scripture quotes to promote their programs, even away from church.

Then the lights came on in the midst of their polar opposite tantrum
No bible verses need be advised from whence hate takes precedence over love
Even without any agitation, cream comes to the top, see the bruises
All it took was a different audience, not the one she speaks of
How the blame game was retrieved to justify their failures and shortcomings.

M. A. GRAYSON

Time to hand out awards for who you really are, if I knew which one would
show up
But in the fullness of time, I'd like to offer the hand of peace in spite of
That you might become one with yourself and gain inner peace, halt
Mercy, mercy me and even more to you, as I pass you the award
Because I can see you have issues, the great conflict with your alter at home.

CHAPTER 72

DENIED A CHANCE

Confined to mom's old inherited home, even in his adulthood
Stunted by the confinements of what his bedroom can hold
He's proud that he surpassed his younger healthy brother that still sleeps
with mom
Both in their late thirties, and other than work, home is all they've fathomed.
Except a seldom quick stop to pay bills or into a store to replenish his snacks, he's
home.

Dad walked out when they were still pups, preschoolers, never to be heard from
again.
There's a question as to whether mom won the debate or dad
Neglecting what's important is the kids lost for lack of instillation and balance?
When now we see days, dogs better dressed, fed, and get far more attention
People identified by numbers and children neglected beyond what the parent can
gain.

In his few conversations away from home, he's infrequently oblique in
presentation
Ever darting eyes that seldom make contact with the person he's chatting with
Most consider him shyly strange at best, but not offensive
Even at home, he peeks his head out of his door to run grab a plate of crumbs
Amazing what the microwave and electronic games have helped create.

Where you find most people dropping names and spitting out stats to build clout
Maybe to get a foot in the door or impress others
Where you find people with small feet trying to wear big boots, overbalanced
Or the large feet in a small sandal, underachievers
But even in volume and style, shoes have a way of personally defining.

Not him, though, as he throws on his wrinkled clean work clothes
Only having another game level advancement to look forward to when he gets
off work
Or get caught up in the new reality show prior to falling asleep for the night
But if one drives by his bedroom window late at night, they can hear
Chuckles from afar, screams of victory, or cries from his heart.
Because even he knows to exit solace can mean to enter novelty.

CHAPTER 73

FINAL DAY

In the midst of a beautiful, bright, and sunny hot summer day
I could feel, I could see it suddenly start getting cold and dark
It's even starting to get hard for me to breathe,
Like my lungs are starving for air as I suffocate.
So, I fight the forces that seem to be trying to overcome my will to live.

In my mind, I hear it's probably best to sit down in this situation
The very good vision I had has been reduced to a cloudy one, at best
I feel a heavy weight in my chest cavity
I compromise with my mind by leaning up against a nearby wall
As I drop my head in deep thought, inquiring, what's happening?

I close my eyes as I consider my next move, and I gasp again; it's getting tougher.
In an environment with no phone reception and not a soul in sight,
I glance down at my watch, but my distorted vision won't allow me to read it.
So, I drop my head again, as I get from deep, an internal affirmation.
Now, it's all getting clear, even my sight in knowing?

So, I take a very deep breath, reminded this has nothing to do with my health
As that same confidence comes over me, even faith.
The dark starts to clear back to bright, and my body temperature reverts to
normalcy.
I raise my head and head out the door because I need to take a walk for some
fresh air
But more importantly, because it's not my day, it's someone else's?

Just to think, I may be their only resolve, their delay with that same destination?
And whether it's a fatality or not, I'm willing to still extend myself beyond my
reach
And as the heaviness dissipates, I recall everything that happens to me isn't
about me.
Not time for your final day either, so get busy.

Chapter 74

Life's fragile

How often do you hear that and it repeats itself more often, as you ripen
Seeing who outlives who next and studying the obituaries, like it's a new course.
Like the lotto, whose number is going to come up next in fatality?
The things that generate mortality has no respecter of person
As the grim reaper marks off the calendar and looks up your address.

Extremes people go through to be aloof on that roll call
Many just want to look good in exiting, while few take control over their exit
The efforts put in trying to outmaneuver what might take them out, even down
Thinking most reading this are fortunate beyond comprehension, they're reading this
Death doesn't just knock on doors anymore; he pays the note too.

As some inquire, why take the good young folks, as you check your priorities now
Leaving us with the miscreants, inspiring quest of injustice
Where today's bliss becomes tonight's tears in the blink of an eye
Where your deepest emotion gets a rude untimely interruption, awakening even
Love to schedule this at a future date, says death's fragile victims?

So, what date would you really suggest, day after never?
Shock value no matter how that day approaches or how it's dressed
Taken aback in knowledge, knowing the last time was the last time
It's seldom who you would think, even in affliction.
As it defies the test results of bad health, crude vises, and dangerous risk.

Many possessed by death instead of being obsessed with life
Is this a case of utilizing the wrong influences to get the right results?
Or is it utilizing secondary means to get primary results?
Maybe a perfect example of the means justifying your end.
Life is fragile and generally a farfetched concept outside a disheartening report.

CHAPTER 75

MORE THAN CUTE

At first birth, you can only lay there in near silence no matter what you need
Eyes fastened to the various new bright views and hues, learning
Nose absorbing the many floating aromas, taking it all in
Totally dependent on the cares and concerns of their guardians.
Also meaning, what they don't know can hurt you, too?

The same falls true in the maturation process from wherever you spend your time.
The lack thereof comes via the same ventures; as you depart your pristine state.
In time, whether you see yourself as greater than you really are, a pompous pauper
While most see themselves as less than whom they are or can be
But few see themselves as they really are, regardless of the obstacles life presents.

Now, this is the extrapolated nutritional meal you wanted with fat burners.
But to be effective, you will have to exercise to get your integral probity inline
Note that the early influences play a large role in all this!
What's mentally planted has much to do with what eventually grows, including
weeds?
The early focus usually sets a standard that later influences and prioritizes.

Snipers in the bushes are expected, but never from your breakfast nook
Not offended in taking a secondary role and excelling
Your great accomplishments bring the unworthy glory
Unable to separate truth from flattery when it's about you
Unable to separate false statements which should be deterred.

Maybe the ultimate compliment comes in someone just inquiring,
Who are you, or that you've changed?
Knowing that means there has been a transformation
But then the next internalized question is; if it's valid and progressive
Diffusing your doubt with the confidence of refusing to be defined by the weather.

Perception is often based on the temporal while truth has intent injected
Spoken from experience differs from hearing the same
That created imbalance where the insignificant outweighs the means
Evincing your evolution is more about your journey's contributions to the next.
Erudition gained in alien nations inspires more depth, not just in being cute.

Chapter 76

Unfinished Business

Most won't be honest with themselves to this extent; eye opener?
In their process of reaching for the stars, yet settling for arm length control,
Many equate managing and controlling their emotions
By networking with those they can control and manage, often with no ill intent.
Hoping to transcend beyond each other's transparencies without being afflicted.

Suppressed in progress by the mental murder of your mother
Murdered your future by suppressing the rising of your father's spirits, misdirection
As the poisoning influences drive law enforcers awry
Repealing the advancing brainchild that was induced into law
We obviously tread barefooted on hot coals of fire in pursuit of casualness.

Most don't know your beginning; maybe have a hint
Most don't know the locale, nor the intensity of your travail
Most don't know your history, clawing officiously.
The rest don't know your walk, let alone your journey, the disconnect
So how do they know you today?

M. A. Grayson

If they don't know your beginning
How do they know your preciosity?
If they don't know your struggle, they disengage
How can they feel your pain?
So how do they know where you're coming from?

Are we capable of exchanging empathy in ignorance?
Do we hyperextend without a sincere heart to heart?
Can we even comprehend our own boundaries, especially without arrival?
All in knowing veritable identical experiences by one,
Isn't viewed the same by another, the disclaimer.

Just like politics started with good intent, yet gone sour
Some messages are only as good as where you've been
As broken promises usually lead to a broken heart, the lemon law.
Resonates an expression with no inflection imposes no intent
So don't turn your back on me now.

CHAPTER 77

NEVER PLANNED

I never planned to get this tired, but just how things turned out.
I work hard and seldom play; I do more than what's expected in epic proportions.
But now I can see, in the lessons revealed, that we do change when fatigued.
Yes, we brush our teeth and put on strong faces to repel doubters questioning.
Rising to the occasion to defeat all comers, as the rest wouldn't consider
challenging.

Unlike most, I never planned to visit my own depths, not because I'm scared.
Just know that I can't change yesteryear or the day before that rehearsal,
Since it didn't kill me, maybe it strengthened me?
Then I wonder is that really strength, efficiently prioritizing my options
Or am I second-guessing myself, again, in selflessness or am I drunk?

I never planned to excel or be great or climb the highest mountain.
It just happened to be in the way of where I was going.
It turned out it was all part of my journey, bearing my counterparts onus.
Some call it fate and yet I still call it just another busy street crossing.
Where timing can be essential in a successful transition.

M. A. Grayson

I never planned to achieve better than my peers and beyond my skeptics.
I've resisted the tackling forces that I've witnessed bring down my predecessors
Where many are prompted to work harder only after the incentive notice,
The wailing from within just not to tip their hand.
The great disconnect was sheer addiction to starvation.

I always planned everything else until spontaneity slipped me a mickey
Which may be why I never plan near as much, now
Because somewhere those uncertainties gave me a newfound respect for
randomness
Opened my eyes to reveal my open-mindedness wasn't as liberal as I thought
As I adjust and clear off my congested calendar for an open day.

CHAPTER 78

THE HURDLES WITHIN

The Neanderthal principle to counteract threats with violence is sophomoric
at best
But when it afflicts heart concerns, maybe even your babies, we disconnect
Knowing that still is a farfetched excuse for a plea of insanity,
You can't seem to execute or locate a more rational remedy
Delegating foolish demands from the seat of your highness.

The things that cause you to speak in tongues of craziness
Make you act outside yourself with no recollection
Make you have a look of loss beyond your companion's recognition
Make you appear uncommonly distant during your daily jog
Just to regain what you generally see as another boring day.

For today, boring can be a beautiful thing after yesterday's adventures
The manner we take our troubles to exponential levels with just questioning
Causing you to look for insight that only leads to disappointments
The manner, the efforts made to return to the calm of breathing rhythmically
The views, the afterthoughts that are generated by these misnomers advance death.

As most give higher value to the detrimental, while the blessings depreciate
The clash of the genders in a foreign understanding of simplicity
The clash of who has to be right over what's right
The indifferences of the insecure debating their own wherewithal
Then deflecting that debate to become another's issue.

Intensifying the light brought on to reflect a sounder path
Often adjusted to condemn the just in order to lower the heating bill
Like many days in which feel better options overcome reason and right
A place where reality is suffocated in extremism
And the bigger voice chauffeurs the sensible without consent, without direction.

CHAPTER 79

HEALING PAIN

Picking up the pure soul full of undeserved, unwarranted afflictions
Swallowing the bitterness in neglecting my necessities, again?
Even though I'm damaged beyond reconstruction, insignificant relays
I've blown off the usual casual intolerances in ascension
Shaken off the behind your back mistreatments and misjudgments.

What most look for in the highest standards were never recognized when I resided there.
Turned a deaf ear to the closet spoken abuses and never forwarded my awareness
The uncalled for character assassinations to elevate their depleted accomplishments
Applying healing dressing to the broken glass hearts, even the deflated was primary
Dispelling self-pity and degradation, culprits of the rise to see another beautiful day.

Where the quiet moments are saturated with rejuvenation and depths driven smile
That opportunity to recover, to glow in satisfaction of equitable achievements
Where preparing for the next battle becomes both natural and simple
But now that there is snow on the roof and shingles missing
Disclosures and direction have become aplenty, painlessly simplified.

Comprehending why pain has to beget displaced pain seems so sophomoric
Convoluted in how the math isn't so easy where generosity is applied
The politics of an oligarchy still influences beyond righteousness

o, point that finger elsewhere because deep down inside,
The conclusion will reveal itself when eyes are closed, as whispers can't find ears.

An awkward silence chills the room in the final moments of the condemned
Praying for rain to wet the parched tongue wishing to spit procrastinated appreciations
Things tough to speak today when it's easy to ask, why me?
No problem regurgitating the tart, yet not enough gratitude for the delicious gestures
Roaming back into a land where helping hands reluctance inconveniently excuses me.
Where healing pains sources just don't quiet the tears.

CHAPTER 80

OFF THE RECORD

Where do you go when the unexpected pulls in your driveway?
Generally, they don't care about you until their moment of need, or is it yours?
Take away the timely presents during their day of celebration
Subtract the kind and encouraging words provided when they're downtrodden
Extract the unconditional support, diluting more than your blood thinners.
Now, what do you have left in this callous cynical world?

Many would respond, blood enthralls an undiluted truth from unbridled lips
A five-star dual-directional piercing, opening up both old and new anxieties
But the recoup advances exponentially, even beyond what meets the eye
Those exceptional expectations completed in mute mode
While the elite choke over their own shouts of conquest, cloaking errs.

Their intent may not be to abuse, but that's the result of their plan
The failing conclusion of distraction not thought through its duration
Another high demand for the pious, the few that consistently deliver
The reps of my house make the laws, set standards and break records
Look forward, even thrive to experience a more perfect challenge of variety.

Mentally disconnected from obtruding into the light of purpose
Pacified in convoluted costive present-day events as opposed to perspiring
So why not just step on the misinformed with judgments of impracticality
Why not just throw the underdeveloped and underprivileged in the undercurrent?
From prowess to predator, if they can't drive, let them suffer, I mean walk.

Why should you have to vanish or alter when they come to your doorstep?
Why should you have to burden the care of others, especially on your sunny day?
Of course, that's out of line, maybe even uncomfortable, but off the record.

CHAPTER 81

WATER OR A WORD

Sensitive to her tears, as fear started to exude through her emotional pores
Out of character, once full of life and zest, even on a bad day
That same character that you never expected to be deflated and conquered
Ever so distant to those that are unfamiliar with tribal language
The day internal revival ceased and desisted, no longer escaping, now on rock bottom.

A residence where the deep-seated partisanships surface and weaken the mighty
Maybe to the common eye, maybe the common perception, maybe not
Maybe they never were mighty, just lost from self-redemption.
Maybe they were just as strong as their seldom revealed weaknesses.
Now, this is getting good, but the point is what's relevant.

In spite of popular opinion, which doesn't equate to apical validity
Nor is it what most fall for in a delectable verisimilitude
Motivation and inspiration is generally for those that climb or thirst
While the rest generally seldom ever give it thought, uncouthly seeking a prize
Except for a few nomads, like you and I, that apathetically just glide.

Then there's the luxury tax that never seems to fit, let alone appeal
When bottom rung luxury differs from the top shelf, even in dust dressing
A good meal, cold drink, and basic subsistence to many is a luxury
To my readers, as they laugh, it's the shiny, the technical, or a nice handbag
The rest its power, size, volume but almost never, Water or a word.
Just let the phone ring, but heed to the call.

CHAPTER 82

FIGHTING AGAINST MYSELF

So, what's real can be derived from many splendored thing.
Yet first, I must recede from whence this all commenced in you.
An appreciation for the never possessed glitter, beyond window shopping
Or an escape back to yesteryears seldom occasions of delight,
For which both have credentials that escalate you felicitously.

Given so many reasons to love even though most failed.
So many types of presented love to choose from, not just an appetizer
Yet in it all, the conclusion, same results claim the jaded
Cries aloud in action with a subtle, very late extension
Clings on for love or the fear of losing it.

Influencing images from afar with unrecognizable feature
But recognizable character that consoles the dark ignorance
Pacifies the night frights in a losing fight
For half a story doesn't make a book
That recurring vicious cycle that emphasizes, humor me.

But the mainstay has its focus on the bleak
Challenged by how much more conflict will I have to tolerate
To gain the patience to applaud self-effort and accomplishments
The endurance of ascending expectations
Suppression of the generational and genetic predisposition to mimic.

M. A. GRAYSON

Pressed by the smell of exaggeration in those driven by fear
Facing my own ugliness in the mirror, greater than a mere reflection
Prioritizing all the ducks that got out of the row
Even the one that humbled me, empathizing with her in time of displacement
Where failure was a consideration, my will inflicted it as not an option.
Now, where's the Welcome mat?

CHAPTER 83

VICTORY QUELL

Strategies to overcome your ally's anxieties that grew you to stardom
Unbeknownst to the offenses in lingering ignorance will hurt you over the long haul.
Engulfed by the gulf of can't and restrained by the undeserving cuffs of learned self-doubt.
Another generational affliction that impedes a sunny tomorrow, dream killer.
Not only for the benefactor but also in detaching.

The many paralyzed in voluntary parental stupidity, even to their cronies.
Finding it difficult to realize and detach from the very arms that offer love
Not comprehending that love is only as good as its progressive unselfish deeds
Consuming the applicable lessons even when it's the polar opposite of lessons given
And no, your mind isn't playing tricks on you.

The comforts of being a failure at home
Caught up in mastering rebellion to following suit and aspirations for your departure
The agony of accomplishments as you deter panache
Knowing you're traveling a lonely road without support
As your peoples' voices sing in unison hate, fear, and if I couldn't, why you?

Never coming to the understanding that silence doesn't equate to not knowing
Others aren't restricted to your incompetent frailties
Others aren't going to allow your failures to dictate their destiny
Others may be grounded by your walk but not grounded to your walk
It's that time where second nature choices become uncalculated.

Asking yourself in evaluation can bad come from good
Asking, can good come from misdirection in spite of proper intent
Take the lesson and take the fall or escape in throwing caution into a prevailing
wind
As hunger drives men and who they'll devour for their prize
Retrospection repels you back to your innocent adolescence in disgust.

The rewarding spoils in victory can quell that overwhelming thirst.

Chapter 84

Victim Benefits

Her childhood skipped far too many stages, an adult way before her time
Trying ever so often to sing her way through the starless nights, no silver lining in sight
Wishing for things that make so many proud and brag of her, even in shallowness
Searching for compliments from any source, but they just don't seem to exist.
Assuming her struggle is original, like brand new?

Volumes of words expressed with a flamboyant glee or even in squelch
Volumes of words expressed in the same similitude, others misread in selfishness
Volumes of words expressed for a simple selfish profit, disguised as some deathly need?
Volumes of words expressed with reception in mind, presented as a favor to her.
With what do I get being the overlooked driving receptive denominator?

Eyes see outwardly, with little regard to inwardly except when transparent?
For what would you look like isn't a factor, when you know who you are, without attire!
Too much to ask or too far advanced to realize inflicting pain won't free you?
Only reenergizes the vicious cycle and often spreads on to the innocent
Never gave it a thought, that sinister benefits never heard her volumes of words.

Not in her graces, as she strengthens salivating the sweet, neglecting bitter aftertaste
Oft condemning lack of physical beauty while harboring an uncomely inclination
As the contagious ugliness breeds a duplicate even from the most gorgeous
Yes, resilience moves past the discomforts, graduates to a lovely day when it's
dreary.
Not waiting until after you've hung up the phone to come up with a kind word.

I want what I want to manipulate and step on others' emotions for my gain?
Hurt me not and make me cry no more, for you know me not, nor my deep silence
Allow me to change my tone in want until my day comes
Allow me to dismiss my fears to aid so many worse off than I, as if they do exist?
Expecting love from one full of hurt that matured into hate, led by my blind
emotions.

Some things don't wash away so easily but can be easier to deal with in time
mindset
Clutch your purse and cling to your cross, your bible, your favorite vise.
And in spite of you closing your eyes, please not your heart, too?
For whatever seems to soothe your soul and pacify the doubtful fears of your mind
Far too often, harsh words have drawn your attention, relishing peace for your own
good.

CHAPTER 85

ADRIFT

Ever trying to define, described in the multi-faceted assumptions
While my endured back pains are just a reminder of your afflictions displaced
Oftentimes, I find myself in the midst of your chaos, ignoring mine that was.
Forever proceeding, while acquiring more answers than inquiries
Way before troubling questions arise, concluding you may not want to recover.

All don't prefer freedom, choosing the comforts of fear and drama as a mainstay
When they see I walk tall with straight back even in the fire, never sweating
Misread by all, yet they want to reside in my broken shoes for a mile
So, I offer my shirt, because unbeknownst to them, I usually walk barefooted
Shoes just hide the sufferings I've bared, while the warmth of a shirt comforts.

Quieting the emotional rage inside like soft music,
Chasing away the nightmares, replacing them with dreams of accomplishments
With no concern of abandoning my familiar for a distant assignment
Like enjoying a home cooked Sunday evening meal with all the trimmings
When it's the small things we dread when the taken for granted dissipates.

Aspiring to quiet deprivation, yet unaware of their self-regard until the 11th hour
So, I get misclassified in their defense because offering a hand tarnishes their jewels
Or maybe it's just because they didn't come up with the idea first
Entangled in their own binding web, which distorts reality
Placing boundaries of trepidation on themselves, hidden by the faults they've
acquired.

Even in the magnitude of all its innocence, I've absorbed the unduly blame before
But I refuse to pay your debts in spite of being nailed to the cross
With all the misfortunes and in my own insignificant way
Just stand up and recognize your own decisions to descend
For no tears will be shed for self-affliction.

As you contemplate, sink or swim, for I've made my claim
But unfortunately, it was for idle adrift for you to drink from the Mason jar
While wisdom encourages you to release your apprehensions.
You elected to dismiss yours in acceptance of a more refined approach
Where the rising of a new sun brings your longing for quietness.

Chapter 86

That Dreaded Subject

Some try to show strong face as their beloved tries to endure their final pains
Most just give up in time with internal expressions of, "No more"?
I've had enough and can't take this any longer as they surrender the ghost.
My time has come as they exasperate that last breath and close their eyes.
The frailty of life and yet the quickness of death from which none are exempt.

The accomplishments and the victories now seem so bland.
The good times, all but forgotten for many.
The bad times regurgitating request for offerings of mercy and forgiveness
And the incidents behind now seem all so minimal.
Energy wasted and time expensed for what?

Time initially went by slow and shortly thereafter excelled at light speed
As the expiration date draws nigh, even for this reader
Many try to retard that day now with crash means of healthy habits
Only to waste more precious time, missing out on more important issues
Overlooking the precious purpose of the taken for granted!

Walking on eggshells while trying to avoid the broken glass
Anxiety rises as that dreaded subject draws nigh
Few appreciate the race for what's meant to be
And many that do almost when it's too late to execute
As the wise belch out, it's not about the gains but giving.

M. A. GRAYSON

Focus has been on what goes in your hand instead of out of your heart,
I believe you're starting to hear the soft music playing, a welcoming alarm?
I know for many, it's the day of separation and deportation,
But for you, just time to go home
Hopefully, for the onlookers and a friend, you gave them reason to live.

CHAPTER 87

BAD BREATH

In a different chapter, yet the same insightful journey, in spite of days gone by,
After surveying the land from various directions,
No longer confusing silence for ignorance nor unresponsiveness for fear,
Some will inconsiderately inflict undue and untrue criticism for self-preservation.

Taking for granted the table that's spread before them in spite of the smell
With disregard for the good in favor of craving for the greedy
Not realizing their integrity is lost somewhere in their wallet,
Slow progressions or eternal optimism as they continue to rock un-tempered
entitlement.

Wondering what's the year of acting your age, outside of adolescence?
Nightmare driven into crowd-pleasing defeats over the fear of lonely success,
Influenced by unwise, selfish directions, as they mull around in indecisive circles.
Where is the anticipation of Friday's a telltale reflecting their true passion?

Saturating your hearing with chimes of biased hate, and spun breaking News.
Digesting parental poisons and temporal occupational dysfunctions,
All for their common good of keeping you handcuffed to a life of reservations.
Not giving forward thought of their reckless disregard for many has caused an
aspirational panic.
But those that escape have had their preceptors trained to review criticism and be
defined by no one.

CHAPTER 88

HIDDEN TEARS OF MY FATHER

They don't always appear just in the lonely dark,
And they're not always about his children or what matters the most,
But his perseverance often drives him beyond what he can attain; some think
Drives him to accept what he can't influence, let alone control?
Desiring the best and accepting many of those results are fulfilled outside his view.

Amazing that he shed them while he was young, in search?
And then came the break from it all, or maybe too busy to recognize.
Now that he's older, the tears of his youth have returned,
But all for a far different reason in his father's eyes,
Because priorities change with maturation if you give time to ponder.

An ever-changing environment has grounded him plus reality
Including the more visible gifting limitations for others.
Challenges that once were a conquerable song
Blues of yesterday successes, even if only in his mind
But today, the musical tones and tempo have slowed to a crawl.
So, he pats his feet to the beat of his own drummer to quench the tears.

www.ingramcontent.com/pod-product-compliance
Lightning Source LLC
Chambersburg PA
CBHW071355120626
46546CB00002B/694